call girl
confidential

call girl confidential

AN ESCORT'S SECRET LIFE

AS AN UNDERCOVER AGENT

rebecca kade

G

gallery books

NEW YORK   LONDON   TORONTO   SYDNEY   NEW DELHI

G

Gallery Books
A Division of Simon & Schuster, Inc.
1230 Avenue of the Americas
New York, NY 10020

NOTE TO READERS
Names and identifying details of some of the people portrayed
in this book have been changed.

First Gallery Books hardcover edition January 2014

GALLERY BOOKS and colophon are registered trademarks
of Simon & Schuster, Inc.

For information about special discounts for bulk purchases,
please contact Simon & Schuster Special Sales at 1-866-506-1949
or business@simonandschuster.com.

The Simon & Schuster Speakers Bureau can bring authors
to your live event. For more information or to book an event,
contact the Simon & Schuster Speakers Bureau at 1-866-248-3049
or visit our website at www.simonspeakers.com.

Interior design by Ruth Lee-Mui
Cover design © Regina Starace
Cover images © Charles Gullung/Gallery Stock; Alex Telfer/Gallery Stock

Manufactured in the United States of America

10 9 8 7 6 5 4 3 2 1

Library of Congress Cataloging-in-Publication Data

Kade, Rebecca.
  Call girl confidential : an escort's secret life as an undercover agent /
Rebecca Kade.
    pages cm
  1. Kade, Rebecca. 2. Prostitutes—New York (State)—New York—Biography.
3. Prostitution—New York (State)—New York. 4. Undercover operations—New
York (State)—New York. 5. Informers—New York (State)—New York. I. Title.
  HQ146.N7K33 2014
  306.74082—dc23
                              2013040743

ISBN 978-1-4767-2681-6
ISBN 978-1-4767-2686-1 (ebook)

To my daughter . . .

whatever you need, whatever it takes.

I love you.

contents

contents

call girl
confidential

I was the call girl who became an undercover operative for the Manhattan district attorney during his investigation of high-class prostitution rings in New York City.

I was a Christian girl raised by strict Baptist parents in a small Southern town where I attended church four days a week. But after a series of events involving a rich criminal, a rocker, and a kidnapping, I needed a tremendous amount of money, and fast. I became a hooker.

I worked as an escort for both "Manhattan Madam" Kristin M. Davis and Anna Gristina, the so-called Soccer Mom Madam. After the DA's swarm of spies stung Anna in 2012, she spent four months in jail and finally pleaded guilty to just one felony count of promoting prostitution. But make no mistake: Anna Gristina ran the most successful high-class call-girl business in New York City for more than a decade, with clients from London to Brunei, and I saw it all up close.

I had billionaires, politicians, CEOs, Wall Streeters, Grammy winners, European luxury moguls, Middle Eastern royalty, and famous restaurateurs among my clients. And when the prosecutors pressed me into service as a confidential informant, they wanted me to continue to have paid sexual encounters with these men.

After Anna was arrested, she maintained a warm-and-fuzzy image for the cameras and joked with reporters and talk-show hosts. But at the height of her game, she hadn't hesitated to send armed enforcers to intimidate a competing pimp who sought to cross her.

Anna had only the most beautiful young women in her employ. One had to audition to work for Anna—unclothed. Girls were chosen not for the surgically enhanced bimbo look of typical escort agencies but for their class and natural beauty. Anna sought out women with an understated elegance who you would never suspect were hookers. A woman who could have a conversation at Per Se with a Wall Street master of the universe just as easily as she could accompany him to a polo match in the Hamptons or a party on a yacht in St. Barts.

Once these men discovered that Anna could provide such introductions, they were hooked, so to speak. They became steady clients who regularly paid thousands for sex and companionship.

New clients at a first session would always vet me by asking how I had met Anna. I never quite knew how to answer that, and tried out many lines that failed to please. But once I said with a sly wink that we had mutual friends, they would relax. I was the girl Anna had promised to deliver. It wasn't a business transaction. I was a friend of a friend, a woman who felt comfortable with her own sexuality as well as his, who enjoyed intimacy for a few hours, no questions asked.

Anna's regular superwealthy clients were happy to share with me that they had known her for many years. Yet, many had never actually met her, and she remained a mystery figure. She operated her business from afar and under the radar. Because of her clandestine methods, Anna was able to run her multimillion-dollar global business without law enforcement having a clue. I believe that it's none of anybody's business what two—or three—consenting adults do. But with my future and my family on the line, I turned my back on Anna and became an undercover operative. It was a decision that would haunt me for years.

worlds collide

An ominous wind blew through Columbus Circle that bitter March day in 2008, and not even the goose-down coat I'd had custom made in London could keep me warm. A shiver cut right through me. I was on my way to forensic psychology class at college, climbing the rungs back to "normal," for myself, for my kid. Well, as normal as I could be with $600 blond highlights and wearing a white cashmere dress and Louis Vuitton heels among a sea of jeans and sneakers. I wasn't trying to show off. I just had to be ready at a text's notice to make an outcall. You see, I had another life apart from being a student. I was what the media calls a "high-class call girl"—someone who makes thousands of dollars an hour just to have sex. A booker might ping me right in the middle of a professor's lecture on the criminal mind that a high-paying client wanted to see me, and off I'd go. I usually let the teacher finish the thought before I left the classroom.

That day, my phone sounded during a lecture on cognition. *Dammit*, I thought, annoyed to be pulled away from class once again. But I looked at my device and saw it wasn't my booker. It was one of the girls I knew when I worked for Kristin Davis, the famed "Manhattan Madam," a true New York character who overindulged herself with plastic surgery and who once ran for governor.

It read, simply: "Go to the nearest newsstand and find the article about Kristin."

That was it. Nothing else. I had not worked for Kristin for some time. I had moved on to a network so sophisticated, it made Kristin's escort service look like child's play. Kristin was sloppy: she accepted gentlemen's credit cards, she ran ads in the adult classifieds, she put everything into her computer. She sprinkled clues like Hansel and Gretel.

Had Kristin been arrested? My friend hadn't texted me any details for a reason, and I was guessing that was because the article had something to do with an arrest. We all knew better than to text anything about criminal issues. Sex Business 101: Don't leave a trail.

My heart was fluttering like a butterfly. I didn't work for her anymore, so why should I be nervous? But my rationale was ridiculous: of course I should be worried. If Kristin kept her old records on her hard drive, I had everything to lose: my daughter.

I took a deep breath, excused myself from class, and took only my phone and purse with me, totally forgetting about the cold.

I ran down to the deli and found it in the *New York Times,* of all places: $2 MILLION BAIL SET FOR WOMAN IN BROTHEL CASE. There was a photo of Kristin. She was on her way to solitary on Rikers Island after being charged with promoting prostitution and money laundering. Cops had found $476,000 in cash in her apartment. They also found her black books, which contained the names of 10,000 men, including celebrities, athletes, and elected officials. As the *New York Post* emblazoned across its front page days later with the headline BUSTED and a photo of Kristin with her ample implants spilling out, New York governor Eliot Spitzer had been one of her clients. (To be more specific, Spitzer had been one of my clients. He had just resigned three weeks earlier after getting caught with another prostitution ring.) The black books contained all the details of the clients' sexual proclivities and what girls they liked. There was no way my name wasn't on Spitzer's "page." I ran out of the deli and could go no farther. Despite my white dress, I leaned against the storefront and sank right down to the sidewalk. I felt as if something was crushing my body and not letting go. I couldn't breathe. The day I had dreaded for years had finally come.

I called my big sister. She had kept the secret of my liaisons with politicians, despite being a high-level Republican aide herself. She had protected me, and now she answered my call in her office on Capitol Hill.

"Bridget," I said through tears. "It happened."

She knew exactly what I meant. I told her the details of Kristin's arrest, and that cops might come after me. Ever since our parents left us to fend for ourselves as teens, she had been my only true confidante. Bridget didn't condone what I did for a living. In fact, she hated everything about it. She could have freaked out, thinking somehow her ties to me would be revealed. Instead, she tried to console me.

"Rebecca, it's going to be all right," Bridget said. "No matter what happens from this moment forward, tell the truth. If anyone from law enforcement comes after you, we will deal with it, but you cannot lie. Never."

I wasn't even telling her the truth. Not completely. Yes, I had told her I had left Kristin's high-priced call-girl agency long ago. What I left out was that I had moved on to an even more wired and therefore more lucrative madam: Anna Gristina. My sister assumed I had left the business.

"Now pull yourself together," Bridget ordered. "Go back to class and act as if nothing has happened."

On my way back to class, I noticed a few gentlemen in suits with badges around their necks standing outside the doorway, talking among themselves, and I got spooked. *Don't be paranoid, Rebecca,* I said to myself. *You're studying at a school for criminal justice. There are always cops and agents all over the place, coming in to talk to classes. Some are even professors.*

Still, I had never seen them before. My footsteps echoed loud and leaden in the corridor, and when I pushed the heavy class-room door, it opened with a loud squeak. As I rushed to my seat I heard my grandfather's voice in my head say, *That door sure needs some WD-40,* and then he would get up and fix it. I wished he was there at that moment to save me and keep that door from making that sound when I opened it. Everything seemed heavier and louder, and I felt as if the whole class were staring at me with judgmental eyes, thinking, *We know who you are and what you are, you whore. Now everybody else will know it too. You will be exposed for being the dirty hooker that you are.* Suddenly, my gorgeous clothing and shoes felt cheap. Everything about me felt cheap and worthless, scared and fearful.

When the buzzer over the intercom system went off, announcing the end of class, I jumped. A new fear took hold of me. I did not want to go home. Where would I go? Would the police be there waiting? Would I be arrested? Would I go to jail, and if I did, for how long? *Oh, God, Kristin, why were you so sloppy?* I thought. I would never see my daughter again. The reason I was in this mess was my need to make a lot of money to fight to keep her in the first place. How had everything gone so wrong?

I gathered my things and began to make my way out of the room. Just then a tall, clean-cut man in a perfectly tailored suit approached. Pretty spiffy for a professor or a student, I thought. Maybe he was an administrator.

"Miss Kade?" he asked.

"Yes," I said, a little confused as to how he knew who I was.

"Could I speak with you for a moment?"

"Of course," I said.

"I mean privately," he said. "It's not about school."

I balked and frowned a bit.

"I'm a little busy here," I said.

He reached into his pocket and pulled out what looked like a wallet. He flipped it open, and a gold badge glinted in the fluorescent lights overhead.

Adrenaline surged through my body. My worlds had just collided.

The detective spoke with me briefly. He wanted me to come with him, but when I told him that I had my scheduled time with my daughter, Isabella, he decided to let me go home and be with her. But he told me to report to Manhattan district attorney

Robert Morgenthau's office first thing in the morning. Morgenthau, whose father had been FDR's Treasury secretary and the architect of the New Deal, had ruled Manhattan law enforcement for thirty-four years. He was eighty-nine years old but still sharp and straight as an X-Acto knife.

I couldn't sleep all night. I had been leading a double life for years. I was a single mom, a PTA board member, and an escort. Keeping that a secret is a lot harder than you may think. Switching mentally from "work" mode to Mommy mode made me feel I could physically split into two pieces at any time. I couldn't take any chances that anyone knew. I knew this because there had been people in my life I had trusted who had turned on me with lies and painful actions that could never be taken back. Their actions would continue to hurt my family.

My daughter's father was one of those people. And as a mother, I had learned that when it comes to your children, when you are backed into a corner with no way out, you will do things you never dreamed you were capable of doing to fight for your loved ones. Isabella's father and I were in court over ridiculous accusations that I was an unfit mother and she should not be in my home. He wanted to take her away from me, and I wasn't about to let that happen. No matter what.

why i went to work for manhattan madam kristin davis

Isabella's father is a rock star—let's call him Mike—who never lived with us, yet he paid child support and saw her regularly. One day he simply didn't bring her home. He had kidnapped her, and I soon learned he had moved in court to gain full custody. Mike hired one of the most powerful family law attorneys in New York City—and one of the most expensive. I guess he did the math and thought it was a better deal than paying child support for ten more years. He claimed that a young man I had staying with us temporarily was a danger to our daughter.

Mike had gotten married one month before he went for custody. Ultimately, the marriage lasted less than a year, but his new wife was very close to Isabella—so close that it made me uncomfortable. I cannot deny that his wife loved my daughter. She loved her tremendously. But when the court proceedings began, I truly felt that they wanted to take me out of my daughter's life entirely so Mike's wife could be her new mother.

I fought back hard. They took that as a sign of mental instability; they called me crazy and whatever else fit the agenda at the time. Any mother would have felt the same as I did. When Mike's wife left him, I figured out that he was feeding the lies to everyone. I wasn't perfect, but I wasn't the monster he was making me out to be. (His wife realized this, and I saw how my daughter had relied on her during my absence; Isabella still needed her love, and it would hurt her to lose it. To this day I still encourage the relationship between them, and they are extremely close.) I refused to allow a divorce from Mike and his judgment to hurt my daughter. He blew the situation way out of proportion. Anyone who truly knew me, knew that. But a judge bought his story, and I lost custody of the daughter I had raised alone since birth. She was six years old at the time.

I had seen mega-lawyer Eleanor Alter on television during the Woody Allen case. She had represented Mia Farrow after the filmmaker had an affair with Mia's adopted daughter Soon-Yi Previn, and Alter went after Woody with a vengeance. She won full custody for Mia of their son, Ronan, the only biological child Woody ever had.

I went to see Alter in her office and told her of my plight. She was willing to help—for a price. A very high price.

"My fee is $750 an hour," she told me. I guess she could

easily get that from all the rich moguls in New York dumping their first wives for trophies, and then dumping the trophies for even younger trophy wives. That included time spent on phone calls and paperwork, and for work done by junior attorneys at the firm. I was soon getting legal bills for several thousand dollars at a time, bills that I could not support with my executive assistant's job. These bills were simply to try to hammer out an agreement about holidays and the normal weekday and weekend schedule. I was furious. I was more than furious, because no one knew better than I did that he was just messing with me. He was trying to control me. He didn't really want all those hours with Isabella. He would never and could never honor any agreement we ever put together because of his "traveling" and "touring" schedule. I couldn't hold it against him if his business required him to be away so much, but my point was that it was impossible for him to honor any parental agreement because of this. Isabella was with me all the time, and I was fighting him all the way. He wanted to take special moments away from Isabella and me and start his own. We had traditions that clearly meant nothing to him.

His girlfriends came and went, and so did my money. One court appearance could cost $8,000 or $9,000. The custody hearings could go on for days. I realized that what I was making at my day job wasn't enough. Not even close. I couldn't even cover a single day in court.

I asked my mother for a loan, and told her I'd pay her back. She wouldn't give me any of her money, even for her granddaughter's sake. She claimed she didn't have it. I believed her.

I cashed out my 401(k), my pension, and Isabella's college fund. That was my future and hers, but this was a fight for my daughter's life, and that was what mattered. That money ran out fast too.

I then started selling everything of value in my home on Craigslist and eBay. When the legal bills came, that money, too, evaporated.

I realized I had better do something. I'm not saying I'm proud of it, but while I was on Craigslist, I started looking at ads for a second job. Personal assistants, part-time, anything that would supplement the full-time position I had. What they were paying for these jobs that mostly women took was depressing. I felt defeated.

I had a friend whom I cried and cried to about this. She said, "It looks as if there is no way out. You are going to lose her, and he is going to win."

That really made me mad. When and why had this become about "winning"? My daughter was not a prize that you won at the end of a game. She was my heart, my precious child who for more reasons I can ever list I would do anything for.

I was desperate. I clicked on the category entitled "Models Wanted" and started reading all these ads about how a girl can make thousands of dollars in weeks. Just reply, they said. So many of them were worded very generally in order to skirt the state laws, but I got the picture: anyone making that kind of money every single week is not really a model. Unless you're Gisele Bündchen. And they're not looking for the world's next supermodel on Craigslist.

No, these Craigslist ads were not for models. They were for sex workers. And I answered one of them, fully aware of what I would be asked to do. I dove into the dark side, and it was so near. It was right there on Craigslist, just a few clicks away.

I answered this particular ad because of the way it was

worded. It read that a female who understood and related to her staff ran it. The money would be about $10,000 a week, depending on how hard a girl wanted to work. It was all up to the girl. It said, "Call or email to set up an interview, and please have an understanding of the business." And that is how I met one of the most infamous madams in New York: Kristin Davis.

I went to her apartment in the Corinthian, the tallest residential building in New York City when it was erected in 1988 by developer Bernard Spitzer. Later, I found that ironic when his son and one of my johns, New York governor Eliot Spitzer, was outed as "Client No. 9."

I was very nervous about the appointment. I had no idea what to wear to this kind of job interview. I remember wearing a pair of light-brown pants, a cream-colored blouse, heels, and light makeup, a bit of jewelry. I was meeting her after my day job coming from downtown, and I took the subway in that beautiful outfit—I was that broke.

Kristin swung open the door and welcomed me in in that brassy, outgoing manner of hers, and the first thing that struck me about her was that her breasts were gigantic. She must have worn a 48DD bra. There was no way they weren't implants. She looked as if she'd had major work done on her face as well, even though she claimed to be just thirty-five. But she was extremely nice and seemed far more intelligent than she looked. She'd actually been the vice president of a hedge fund before, shall we say, transitioning careers.

I said I'd just come from my job in the Financial District.

"No problem," she said. "A lot of my girls work on Wall Street."

Her "girls"? I thought. What was I getting myself into?

I guess she was giving me the once-over as well, and I must have passed muster. Boys always seemed to notice me in school. I do have curves, and I've always worked to stay in shape. And the Lord did bless me with straight, light-blond hair, which I wear all the way down to the small of my back. One of my boyfriends once called me Lady Godiva.

I must have seemed as nervous as I felt, because Kristin offered me a glass of wine. She asked me a little bit about myself and then she started to explain the business.

"Are you interested in 'outcall' or 'incall' work?" she asked.

I had no idea what she was talking about. I was completely naïve. She saw that, and chuckled.

"Basically, it is what it sounds like," she said. "I have a nice cozy place, and some of my girls meet gentlemen there. We call those 'incalls.'"

I guess that's what people call a brothel, I thought to myself.

"We also have a lot of clients who like the girl to come over to their own apartment," Kristin continued. "Yes, that's what I said: they have sex right in the same bed they sleep in with their wife. I don't know where the hell the wife is at the time, but we haven't been caught yet. Anyway, that would be their problem.

"Other men prefer hotel rooms. Nice hotel rooms. We're talking the Waldorf, the Pierre, and the Regency. You might go out to dinner with him first, so you have to dress nicely. We call these 'outcalls.'"

Wine or no wine, what Kristin said only made me more nervous. I was raised in a strict Christian home, and I had hardly even had any boyfriends in my life. I got pregnant with Isabella at the early age of twenty-one and had barely dated since. How was I going to go to a room in a fancy hotel and have sex with a complete stranger? What if he wanted to do some kinky thing that would freak me out? What if he tried to hurt me?

Kristin has a big, charismatic personality. She's a little like that legendary speakeasy owner Texas Guinan, who'd greet people in her club by saying, "Hello, suckers!"

Kristin has a very open mind about sex, and thinks our society is way behind other countries. She says that the lawmakers who keep prostitution laws on the books and enforce them are some of her biggest clients. Look at Spitzer. When he was New York State attorney general, he prosecuted a tour company that took men to countries where prostitution is condoned. Kristin calls such pols hypocrites. You may have seen her on TV, calling for prostitution to be legalized. She even ran for governor on that platform.

Kristin cajoled me, trying to allay my fears.

"Look, honey," she said, "if you're going to date men you don't even know that well, like all girls do these days, you might as well be paid for it. And paid well. Do you realize how much my gals are making in a week? One just saved enough to buy herself a racehorse. And with your looks, you could do very well for yourself. How about it?"

Without telling her my reason, I really had no choice. Nobody could help me get my daughter back but me.

"I'll try it," I said meekly.

"That's my girl!" she exulted. "Now let me tell you about my little bag of tricks."

Kristin proceeded to tell me lots of different things that she had taught the other girls to do—things that would make the clients keep coming back for more, and once they were there, things that would stretch the session out, make it go longer, even hours longer. The client would be happy, but so would we, because he would be charged more. That meant more money for Kristin as well as for me, since she would split it with me right down the middle. Kristin was going to take a 50 percent cut of whatever I did.

I wondered: *What will I have in my bag of tricks?*

my first client

Kristin called me within two days.

"OK, girl, are you ready to rock and roll?" she chirped. "I've got somebody nice for you at the Parker Méridien."

Le Parker Méridien! Skylit swimming pool, Central Park views, spa. I used to cut through its columned lobby from West Fifty-Sixth Street to West Fifty-Seventh just for a luxe moment in a harried day. Now I was being asked to go meet a complete stranger there to have sex.

"Room 3606," Kristin continued in businesslike fashion. "Just go right to the elevator casually like you're a guest and up to his room; don't stop by the concierge desk to be announced. His name is Stephen. He sounds like he's got plenty of dough, so take your time."

"Kristin," I mewled. "I don't know if I can do this."

No matter how fancy the hotel or how big the payment, it still felt . . . cheap. If I did it, I would have to get out of this "line of work" as soon as I possibly could.

I was afraid too. I had heard of incidents where escorts had been killed after meeting men online. Kristin knew only a little about "Stephen," and I wondered if she had screened him. Screening is when your boss, your pimp, your madam—whatever you want to call them—makes sure that the person on the other side of that door is who they say they are and that they are safe. Looking back now, again, how does anyone know who is safe, by the sound of their name and their credit card number or which hotel they are staying in? No bodyguard would be going with me to wait just outside the door and listen to make sure everything was all right. I would be totally on my own. And doing God knows what.

I thought about my pastor back home in North Carolina. "Revelation 21:8!" he would fairly holler. "'But the fearful, and unbelieving, and the abominable, and murderers, and whoremongers, and sorcerers, and idolaters, and all liars, shall have their part in the lake which burneth with fire and brimstone: which is the second death.'"

I would find out later that the first death was even closer than I realized. A few months after I started, Kristin's booker, Lucy, began surreptitiously booking us and taking the 50 percent cut for herself. She didn't screen clients at all. She didn't care about us, as long as she got her percentage of the thousands of dollars we would make from one encounter as she sat there and did nothing. One night she sent me to Washington, D.C., where I was truly terrified that I would be badly hurt, if not murdered, like one of those girls you hear about on the news.

"Rebecca, are you there?" asked Kristin. "Look, do you want to do this or not? Because he wants you there at eight o'clock, and if you're not up for this, I've got to call another girl. It's not anything you wouldn't do with your boyfriend; I know this guy enough to know he's not a freak. And by nine o'clock, you'll be a thousand dollars richer."

I had no choice.

"OK," I said. "I'll do it."

"That's my girl! Wear lacy lingerie. He likes that."

Great, I thought. *I have none of that. I will have to go shopping, which means the profit from this encounter will be minimal.* But I had a feeling I would soon be making some real money.

I will never forget that night. One usually goes directly to the gentleman's room; sometimes they even leave a key card for you in a magazine in the lobby. But they were renovating the Parker Méridien, and I had to meet this stranger outside on the sidewalk so he could escort me into the hotel as if we were a couple.

I shivered in the freezing January evening, and as the clock ticked past our appointed hour, I started to get anxious. Had he seen me, changed his mind, and turned on his heel? Maybe I wasn't tall enough, or perhaps he preferred brunettes. I called Lucy and wondered if I had mixed something up. She told me to wait while she called the client to see what the problem was. It seemed an eternity and I called Lucy again. "Where is this guy?" I asked in exasperation. She confirmed the time and place and instructed me to continue to wait and I was not to leave. I was miserable. I was literally standing out on the street, waiting for a john. Is this what I had reduced myself to? At that moment, I did feel like a $20 corner hooker. I felt like running home, but I was already out cab fare and would have to spend more going home, and that was money I could not afford. I was that broke.

Finally, a tall man in his forties approached and said, "Ashley?" (That was the name I'd decided to use.) He apologized profusely, as he had been waiting on the Fifty-Sixth Street side of the hotel. Being from out of town, he didn't know that West Fifty-Seventh Street is one of New York City's main thoroughfares, with Carnegie Hall just steps away. He seemed pleasant enough, but I was still overcome with the feeling of despair that had overtaken me. But I knew he would sense it, so I willed myself to snap out of it.

I tried not to call attention to myself as he led me through the Parker Méridien lobby and I clickety-clacked across the hotel's marble floors in white-and-gold four-inch stilettos. They were still in my closet from my nightclub days, and they matched a tight white dress I had that looked good with my hair. I was all white and virginal, but underneath I had on a thong and lace push-up corset. What kind of job dictates your underwear? The job I was about to begin.

The elevator went up with a whoosh and I tottered down the thickly carpeted hallway with him to Room 3606. My heart was doing a drumroll in my chest.

He unlocked the door and held it open for me. "Well, come in . . ." he said. It was the first time I was able to get a good look at him. He looked fine. He helped me off with my coat. He was making me feel at ease—more of a gentleman than I had expected. He had a big smile, so I guess he liked what he saw. That was a relief. He had a deep voice, and he was wearing charcoal-gray trousers, a French-cuffed shirt, and a fleur-de-lis-patterned tie, a bit loosened. "I'm Stephen," he said. "And did I get it right? Ashley? A beautiful name, befitting a beautiful lady."

Ashley was to be my nom de guerre. From that moment on, until the time I walked out his door, I was the persona Ashley. Rebecca no longer existed. I had to push everything about the real me aside and lock it away in my purse. Who I was, all the things about me that would identify me—the things I really cared about, things I liked—were hidden. I morphed into the woman I thought he wanted. It would become my modus operandi with every client: I had different names and different personalities. It was more for my sake than theirs. If it was all pretend, then it was easier to emerge from afterward. At the time I thought it was more to hide who I was from them so I could keep my identity unknown, but later I would realize that it was most definitely for me. I could not have done this job if I even minutely felt it was the real me. I would "flip the switch." You will hear me say that from time to time, because later I literally had to keep track of how many switches I was flipping at once. But for now, it was my first encounter as Ashley, and I was terrified. I had no idea what to do, really.

I noticed he had a bit of gray at his temples, and he seemed pleasant enough. "Would you like a drink?" he asked.

"Just a Coke, if you have it," I said. What a joke. He could have whatever he wanted at the Parker Méridien. Including, apparently, me.

He had a suite, with a modern Scandinavian dining table, art all over the walls, and a living room overlooking the lights of New York City. It was bigger than my apartment. He led me to the sofa, and I wondered if he could tell if I was nervous.

"You sure you don't want a little Jack Daniel's in your soda?" he asked as he handed it to me. "I thought I detected a drawl, and I know Southern girls like their bourbon."

Did all the other girls drink a lot? I wondered. Did they party, do drugs? Was I supposed to do that too? Kristin hadn't warned me about this. I was never one to get drunk or do drugs, and I was improvising as I went along.

"No, this is fine, thanks," I said, and he proceeded to ask me where I was from, what I was doing in New York. Basically he asked me all about myself, and I chattered on nervously. I didn't tell him I had a daughter. I didn't tell him why I was doing this, and he didn't ask. I asked him about himself, and he said he was with an oil company that was exploring other sources of energy. Not for how it would help the planet, but because it would create other revenue streams for the company. He asked me if I'd heard which shows on Broadway were getting good reviews. He took his time and acted as if he didn't have a care in the world, and he didn't seem to notice that we had been chatting for nearly an hour.

After a little while, though, he did become restless, and I knew that he needed something a bit more entertaining.

"I notice that you brought a bag along with you," he said. "Would you mind sharing what you have in there with me?"

Blood rushed to my face. I knew from Kristin's bag-of-tricks talk that for this client that meant modeling lingerie for him. Kristin had encouraged me to put it on in the bathroom and strut out with the seductive confidence of Sharon Stone in *Basic Instinct*.

I honestly would have preferred to be shot at that moment. I was way too shy. I smiled nervously and slipped off into the marble bathroom and locked the door.

I must have spent fifteen minutes in there, changing. I was terrified.

"Do you need any help in there?" he called. "Or should I just get naked and come in there and we can take a shower together?"

"I'll be right out!" I squeaked.

I unlocked and slowly opened the door. I was wearing a black-and-flesh-colored lace push-up corset and garters with black stockings and five-inch heels. He was extremely pleased. I started to talk flirty and even a little dirty, and he became . . . even happier.

He asked for me to keep it all on and he lifted me off the ground and effortlessly placed me on the bed. He left his shirt and tie on, and I saw that he had begun to sweat. He unbuckled his belt with one hand without looking, and his pants dropped down.

He wasn't wearing any underwear, and I could see how hard he was. And then, after all my anxiety, it was over in less than two minutes.

He finished and threw himself on his back next to me, breathing as if he had just run the New York Marathon.

Then I just got up, picked up my things, and got dressed. He paid me in cash and said, "I hope to see you again on my next trip," as he helped me on with my coat. He led me to the door, and just before I went out he kissed my hand. He was a gentleman—unlike several famous clients I was yet to meet. But I had crossed a line that night. I had lost . . . innocence.

Could I do this again? I asked myself as I descended in the

mirrored elevator, regarding my reflection. I knew I would take a long hot shower when I got home. But I also knew my answer by the time I had hailed a cab. With his generous tip, I had $4,500 in my purse—in cash. The cab ride would be no worry this time. Yes, I would do it again.

I called Kristin as soon as I got into the taxi.

"Wow, you were there for a good long while," she said. "How was it?"

"Different," I replied. "I don't know if I know what I'm doing."

"Oh, you know what you're doing, honey."

"I felt guilty—he had a wedding ring on," I fretted.

"Girl, did you just fall off the turnip truck?" she chided. "Half the men you're going to be with are married. They're faithful to their wives when they're home in East Ashtray, Texas, but when they're on the road, well . . . what their wives don't know won't hurt 'em. I think married movie stars call it a 'location lay'—ha. Listen, he paid you in cash, right?"

"Yes, I have it."

"Good," Kristin said. "You wanna work tomorrow night?"

one of the girls

When I finally got home, I couldn't get the keys in the lock quickly enough. I stripped down completely. I put everything in the washer and jumped into the shower. I was numb. I slid down onto the shower floor, hugging my knees, and cried.

I prayed, *Please, dear God, forgive me.* I cried all night, and I was afraid of God all night. In the morning I snapped out of it when I looked over at my daughter's empty room. *Anything,* I thought. *I will do anything to get her back.*

If the worst thing I do is let others take my body to pay these impossible bills, I will answer to God for that. But she will not suffer because her father wants to go to war with me. I will give everything I have, even my body, myself.

I ran out of funds just a few months after the custody battle began in 2005. Soon I would go to work at my regular day job and then afterward I would work for Kristin. I was working days and working nights, because Isabella was not in my home. She was with him.

I don't think I ever felt comfortable or got used to the idea of working during my time as a call girl with Kristin. Maybe it was the clients, or maybe it was seeing the other girls and how they reacted to the job. Sometimes I couldn't tell if I was crying because I missed Isabella, I was disgusted at myself, I was sad because I felt I was losing in court, or because no matter how hard I worked, it was never enough money. I could feel myself falling apart. There were days when I thought I was truly losing my mind; I would have panic attacks and breathe into a paper bag to try and get myself to calm down. I realized more than ever that I had to separate myself, the girl I truly was, from the girl these men wanted and needed me to be and that I was getting paid to be. The effort it takes to achieve that is nearly impossible but absolutely necessary. It never got easier to do the job. The only thing that got easier was pretending that it didn't bother me and that I loved each and every one of my clients. There is no time for a real life. You go into survival mode. And that is what I did and have done for years.

I would pull all-nighters for Kristin, sometimes working until four or five in the morning, then get a couple of hours of sleep and get to work by 8:30 a.m. Then I'd do it all over again. It was exhausting, but I had to pay the attorneys and the rent on my apartment and buy Isabella things. And I had to look good for my night job, and that cost money. A lot of money.

A regular girl running around New York may think about her manicure and pedicure, her highlights and waxing and even a few extras along the way, but an escort for whom men pay thousands of dollars is at another level of maintenance entirely. The clients expected it. No, they demanded it. I had to make sure my highlights were touched up frequently and had my hair blown out several times a week. I had to be immaculately manicured, pedicured, and waxed. Frequent facials. Eyelashes put on every two weeks, spray tanning every three to four days, so you have that perfect glow and look as though you just returned from St. Barts.

But just as important was my wardrobe. A high-priced escort has to look sexy but elegant as soon as she walks in the hotel-room door or accompanies a client to a party or restaurant. Eventually I collected racks of pretty dresses, several hundred pairs of sexy shoes, and expensive lingerie. Building a beautiful wardrobe takes time and work. And, yes, my regular clients let me buy whatever I wanted on their dime all along Fifth or Madison. But it takes a lot of effort to look *expensive*.

I know what you are thinking: *Oh, poor little you*. But I actually had to view myself as a business in which I was the major investor. Sure, I was pretty, but lots of girls are pretty. I had to be a full-fledged fantasy.

I took some of those initial profits and bought things that would transform me into a woman that the richest men in the world desired, again and again. My outfits could each cost thousands of dollars. I learned quickly that this was a game, and decided I was going to be the queen of it. I had to be if I wanted to make the big bucks.

The work was incredibly risky. Kristin had a knack for getting us a lot of work. But generally a man could call and give a credit card number and he was in. That's all it took to get a booking. He could have been a serial killer for all she knew. And I never knew who I was about to see.

I did some incall work at the apartment Kristin had rented at the Corinthian. She also had a couple of other apartments that she would use as incall locations, and they would always be able to serve two customers at a time. Kristin wouldn't be there most of the time. We girls would come to protect one another and keep each other company in the living room even if we weren't scheduled to work. We stuck together.

There were beautiful girls from all over the country and from all over the world, fate having brought them into this line of work for any number of reasons.

There was a beautiful Ukrainian girl whom I'll call Ekaterina—Kit Kat. I really, really liked her a lot. She was extremely intelligent and we could talk for hours. I always respected her because she knew this job served a purpose, unlike some of the others. Her family was from Chernobyl, and although she hadn't yet been born when the nuclear power plant disaster happened there, her sisters had, and they were very sick. One of them had thyroid cancer. Kit Kat sent money back to her mother and sisters every month. They thought it was pay from the job she also had at a well-known public relations firm. She was like me, working days and nights. She made good money, but it was nothing compared to what she got at night, even after Kristin took half. Her public relations coworkers had no idea. She, too, hated the work at the Corinthian, but it was a means to an end, and she would do whatever it took to help her family. She was perhaps one of the strongest women I have ever met in my entire life. After I stopped working for Kristin, Kit Kat and I would meet for dinner or lunch just to make sure the other was OK. She was one of the few who knew my true story. She is also the one who sent me the text to read the article in the paper about Kristin's arrest. I never heard from her again. I hope she is well.

Some of the girls didn't have a serious purpose like Kit Kat. In fact, a lot of the girls spent all their money on clothes, bags, and vacations. They would pay their rent and then blow the rest on the next Louis Vuitton bag. It was refreshing to be around them every once in a while because of their airhead mentality and total ignorance of the seriousness of our life-altering stress. But it also made us feel sorry for them, because they fell for the clients who would say, "Hey, let's go out to dinner" and "I really want to take you shopping." Translation: *Let me get sex for free, and you will never see it coming—and then you will get fired for seeing a client outside of the business and be out of a job.* We always warned them, but they never wanted to listen. And it always happened.

There was Allie. She was always falling in love. She was really good at her job. She was a little wild, but she had amazing natural breasts that made her a favorite of some of the clients. So, even though she was a little plain, those breasts were enough to keep her employed. We weren't allowed to smoke or drink if we were at the Corinthian, but Allie did all the time, like it was a party. She was a student but she'd drop out all the time, then go back and then quit again.

Then there was Lizzie, a very young girl from Minnesota who was a bit of a pathological liar. Actually, let me correct that: she was an outrageous pathological liar. If she wanted to see her boyfriend one night and didn't want to work, she'd just say her grandmother died, forgetting that she'd told Kristin her grandmother had died the month before. Kristin wasn't stupid and always knew what she was up to. One day Lizzie said her sister died. Truly horrible. I am not sure it gets worse than that. I felt really sorry for her, but before I knew how much of a liar she really was (because all of the girls wanted to get out of schedules), we were actually pretty decent social friends. Notice I said "social friends." Not close, but social. I always keep people at just the right distance to be safe. Oh, and to be clear: her sister did not pass away.

One night Lizzie asked me if I would do her a favor and come along on a job at the Waldorf Astoria. She had been working for many different madams. I didn't know her other madam this time, but the job seemed very simple: she needed another girl to come along to socialize at a party, and we would be paid to mingle. Easy enough. She said it was an easy job, so I had no problem doing that.

A well-known media executive and his friends were throwing the party; that was all she knew at the time. We were told to wait downstairs in the lobby, where we would be greeted and then taken up to the apartment. We went up, and the apartment had a beautiful ornate door. When it opened, we walked in, and Lizzie and I were escorted over to the enormous dining area. I introduced myself and my friend to the others in the room. It was a bit confusing, because we had been told we were going to a big party, and there were only about four or five people in the room. We shrugged it off, as champagne was flowing and servers were bringing out hors d'oeuvres of oysters and shrimp.

One of the guests poured me a drink and asked me my name, and I replied, "Why, my name is Ashley," and smiled with my usual wink and giggle. It always puts someone at ease when I amp up my Southern accent. His eyes immediately brightened, and he said, "You are a Southern girl!" He said he was Dr. Benjamin Chavis and that he was also from North Carolina. He had been the head of the NAACP and now directed the Hip-Hop Summit Action Network. We had a lot to talk about.

Our client was the host of the party. There were framed photos of his family all around the apartment. Lizzie and I just mingled among the guests. Dr. Chavis and I talked all night. I never got the sense he wanted to "avail himself of the services," though he did give me his cell number. He explained that a number of them were being inducted as ambassadors to the UN for something the next day and this was a mini celebration, without their wives and girlfriends. Ambassadors for what, I didn't ask, but I acted as if I was impressed. That was my job.

By the end of the night, nothing sexual had happened. We were prepared for it, but it just ended up being a straight party. But the client did not want to pay. He said, "I am not paying for you to hang out and talk and eat hors d'oeuvres."

"Oh, no, no, no, no," I insisted. "No one's leaving this apartment till you pay. Not any of your friends, not Dr. Chavis, no one is leaving until you pay."

"I don't have any cash on me," he said.

"So send your bodyguard now," I snapped.

"Jay-Z's waiting for us," he pleaded. "We have to go to the 40/40 Club. I don't carry cash."

"Too bad," I said. "You'd better go get some. You know full well why I'm here. This is a business transaction. You have to pay us whether you have partaken or not. You see this girl? She has to answer to somebody. She is going to get into a lot of trouble. Do you really want her to possibly get hurt?" I looked over to Lizzie. She wasn't doing anything to try to get this money; I didn't know who had set this job up, but what I did know was Lizzie had better get their cut. I didn't want to see Lizzie get hurt. I had no idea who she had gotten herself mixed up with, if these were the types of clients being sent her way.

They all said, "We're leaving."

I said, "Really? Here's what's going to happen. We're all going to go downstairs. If that money is not there at the concierge desk by eight a.m., I have taken pictures of all of you in this apartment without you knowing, and I am going to put every single one of you online as having been with us. Welcome to New York."

The money was there in full and on time.

Oh, a postscript on Lizzie: I did her that favor, and later she stole $3,000 from me. I never heard from her again.

Many of the girls had boyfriends; some were even married. They were usually pretty open about it among the other girls. But most of their boyfriends or husbands didn't know what they did. They'd have to conceal their lingerie and condoms. Their boyfriends were definitely not seeing that when they got home. I never talked about Mike, and I was terrified somebody would find out who he was. Or had been.

There were some very famous models that worked for Kristin. Girls who'd been on the cover of *Vogue*, *Elle*, *Harper's Bazaar*, *Cosmopolitan*. They usually did outcalls. But occasionally they would pop in to meet a client at Kristin's place and their attitudes were above and beyond atrocious. They behaved as if they were better than we were, even though they were putting their stilettos up in the air just the same.

We girls would talk about clients too. We would say this guy likes this and that guy likes that. Or we might say, "Watch out for that guy." We would share tips. And if we didn't like somebody, there were always tricks to get him to finish quickly. We made sure the new girls never let a guy talk them into "bare backing." Bare backing is sex without a condom. Any type of sex, including oral.

Some girls wanted to see how many clients they could have in a day. I don't understand why they would ever want to do that. I guess they got competitive with each other. You know, as if they were trying to say that they were the most popular girl in school.

I was making a lot of money with Kristin, but ultimately I just couldn't put up with her surprises anymore. Her vetting process was atrocious; no, it was nonexistent. Whether it was New York, Boston, Philadelphia, D.C., it didn't matter: you never knew who was walking in the door or who you were going to see. Unless it was one of your regular clients.

Aside from the obvious risk factors, I liked to know who it was I was going to see, because I needed to know who I was going to be. I had different personalities with different people, and I went by several names. My psyche had to change because of who each man was and what his needs were. If I went into something blind, I didn't know who I needed to be for that person.

And, of course, with no bodyguards, no security, and no bookers present, not even Kristin there, you were meeting complete strangers and having sex with them. Physically, they were bigger and stronger. Anything could have happened. It was very dangerous work. There was always a feeling of risk.

It was time to move on. But as I would eventually learn, I was in deeper than I had realized.

rock star daddy

Are you wondering how I could have sex with strangers for money? No matter how desperately I needed cash to get my daughter back? Are you still judging me? Calling me all the lowest names a woman in our society can be called? Thinking you could never do it?

Perhaps if you knew that the man I was fighting against for custody of my daughter was a rock star with unlimited funds—or so I thought—then maybe you would understand. When he kidnapped our daughter, I vowed I would do anything I could to get her back.

I met Mike at a party for a childhood friend of mine. Bob Guccione had just made her his Penthouse Pet of the Year.

Quite buxom and a natural blonde, my pal was known to Guccione and to her fans as Paige Summers. But back in the tiny Bible Belt town where we grew up, I knew her as Nancy Ann Coursey. Nancy was my dearest friend before I left my hometown. She understood the harsh way my sister and I were being raised.

We grew up in Morganton, North Carolina, which few people know is the site of the first European settlement in the U.S. interior, built forty years before Jamestown. But it was also a hotbed of the Ku Klux Klan. My father was a very stern and scary man to me growing up, and he ruled our house with an iron fist.

He worked at the state psychiatric hospital, and every day when he came home, he would go into the yard and shoot his BB gun at squirrels. He beat my sister and me for the tiniest infractions with switches that we would have to pick out ourselves. I called it "pick a switch." I hated it; I knew I had to be careful because you didn't want to pick a big one that would be too harmful, but you also didn't want to pick one that was too small. Coming back with a small one would result in him becoming angrier and going to get his own or getting out the belt.

In the house, even at dinner, he forced us to be absolutely silent. He didn't want anyone talking about much of anything, really. My sister and I hid in our room and whispered and kept to ourselves a lot. We would spend our time before he came home from work building pine-needle forts in our backyard. But once he was home, we had to come inside as well—only to go about our homework and chores in silence.

Our parents got together with other like-minded parents and

collectively taught us at The Children's School. We didn't go to school with all the other kids in town. This isolated us even more. We were not allowed to watch television—not that we had one, anyway—and our little school didn't have a gym. I yearned to take gymnastics or dance lessons. My only extracurricular activities were attending the Baptist church three nights a week and all day Sunday—whether it was for choir or hand bell rehearsal or Bible study—and music. My father played the dulcimer and some brass instruments and insisted my sister and I practice classical music on ours—she on the trumpet and me on the trombone and violin—for hours.

At the time, I would pray while walking to church that I would be kidnapped and go live with a family that was different from ours. But one day, after years of torment, it all suddenly ceased.

When I was thirteen my father was diagnosed with a brain tumor that had gone undiscovered for years. Perhaps that is why all his behavior towards us was so harsh when we were children. He had surgery to remove it, but there was good and bad news at the same time. The tumor was successfully removed, but he would have severe memory loss and lose some other abilities as well, and he was shipped off to a rehabilitation center, hours away, where he would live for the next couple of years. My mother simply up and left us for what felt like most of the time. She moved to the apartment offered to family members where my father had been sent for rehabilitation, claiming that she needed to oversee his care.

For the most part, she left my fourteen-year-old sister to finish raising me. And once that happened, everything changed. We went to the junior high school in town. We didn't go to church four days a week anymore. We could have friends come into our house for the first time, without fear.

But not before the most amazing thing happened, especially for two girls who had lived in such a strict household. My mother sent us to Europe. She had planned this trip for all four of us. The air tickets were nonrefundable; the hotel reservations had been made. "Go," she told us. "Your father would want you to. Here's the itinerary."

So, at the ages of thirteen and fourteen, we were suddenly set free on another continent. My sister led me through Paris, London, Switzerland, and the Netherlands. I remember visiting Anne Frank's house with sadness; going to see the rock musical *Starlight Express*; skiing on Mount Jungfrau; and walking through the beautiful fields of flowers back to the Hotel Regina in Wengen, Switzerland.

After growing up in a virtual prison, here we were, teenagers trekking around Europe, managing our bags, catching planes, checking into hotels, ordering dinner. Never once were we questioned. Perhaps European concierges are used to boarding-school students; perhaps they thought we would soon meet up with our parents. My mother didn't seem to worry about us, as she was solely focused on our father. She had always been about serving our father, and we were on our own away from our parents for the first time. We were only too ecstatic to have freedom, and after observing the haute life of Europe, I yearned for more. And when I got back, it seemed that my friend Nancy Ann did too.

Nancy Ann was the daughter of a farmer, and she blossomed early into a very voluptuous girl. Married men went after her and told her they loved her, but she did not succumb to their promises. She was very smart in that particular department. They would give her things. I watched it happen. I watched it happen in high school. Men wanted her and would do anything and give anything to get her attention.

She started working as a stripper in a nearby town. I didn't judge her as so many in town did. Only God can judge. I offered my friendship, but others were not that way, and one affair caused such a scandal that she fled. Eventually she ended up in New York City. I had already done the same thing.

"You'll come home in a body bag," my mother had warned jokingly when I left town at age twenty, just one week after my birthday.

Nancy Ann soon started modeling for *Penthouse* magazine as the featured centerfold, and then she was named *Penthouse* Pet of the Year. She called me. *Penthouse* owner Bob Guccione, who owned a mansion on the Upper East Side with a swimming pool inside surrounded by ancient Roman statuary, wanted to throw her a party. It was to be at the Chaos nightclub, and Nancy Ann pleaded, "Won't you please come? I won't know anybody!" I told her of course I would. I had just turned twenty-one and would be allowed in.

I wasn't sure what to wear to such an event, but a fashionista friend of mine who'd been in New York City longer went through her closet full of frocks. We decided on a long silver gown with a velvet bodice.

Inside the club, there was a VIP area. "Do not let anyone sit here," Nancy Ann sternly warned me. She didn't want the usual gaggle of guys drooling over her on her special night. As we sat on a couch together observing the ogling men and giggling, I noticed she had a man's name tattooed on her ring finger. She was dating a photographer and she said they were engaged. Nancy

Ann was always going to marry someone. So the men were kept at bay.

But then a man with longish hair, definitely older than I was, came into the VIP area, and for some reason Nancy Ann let him sit with us. I had no idea who he was. You see, because of the way I was raised, my sister and I weren't allowed to watch TV until after my father had gotten sick, so I missed most of the music, movies, and TV shows of my generation, and I had never seen a music video in my home. I had seen them at a friend's house. The only songs I knew were hymns and classical music, for the most part. I was a girl who didn't "get" so many pop-culture references: people would mention movies, TV shows, actors I'd never heard of; they'd use catchphrases like "Excuuuuse me!" and everybody else would laugh and I wouldn't know why. Sure, I was learning a lot being in New York now, but I had a lot to catch up on.

We started talking. He was ten years older—I was twenty-one—and I didn't find him particularly handsome. But he was very gentlemanly. He had impeccable manners. I did have a thing about manners. I had been used to guys hitting on me since I was fifteen. Other guys are always in your face, bragging about what they do. Mike wasn't doing that. I do think he assumed I knew who he was. But I had no clue. Nancy had decided to leave, and he asked me out on a date. When we spoke on the phone a couple days later, he asked me, "What would you like to do? What are you interested in?" I was taken aback. I didn't know; I was new to the city.

He said, "I know what we should do." I was relieved, and it was nice that he was taking the initiative by making a plan and not making me struggle to help figure one out. But it also meant I was at the mercy of his tastes.

That night, he took me to the Blue Note on West Third Street in the Village to see McCoy Tyner. That was our first date. I remember wearing a long black skirt and a white jacket that I thought was cool at the time. Now I would be so embarrassed to be seen in it, but I had no sense of fashion. He never said anything about it. But at age twenty-one, a night of jazz at the Blue Note was definitely not my thing. In retrospect, I'm sure Mr. Tyner was great. But I wasn't ready for it. This was not the right date for us. It should have been a clue for me: he was tone-deaf to anything I might really have enjoyed. Yet, he called and he wanted to go out again. I was twenty-one, in perfect shape, with natural light-blond hair to my hips. Gee, I wonder what he wanted . . .

He asked me to dinner. He took me to Cent'Anni on Carmine Street in the West Village. I had never been to a really nice restaurant before. When we walked in, it was obvious they knew him, but I thought it was just because he went there often. And this was partly true.

"What are you in the mood for?" the waiter asked. "We will make whatever you like, because you are our special guests."

I had never eaten off a menu in my life. Mike encouraged me to have whatever I wanted, and before long they brought me the thickest veal chops I had ever seen. The lighting was subtle, and the waitstaff made us feel that we were the center of the universe.

The next time, he brought me to a dive bar on the Lower East Side—the self-consciously hip thing to do—but for him it was slumming, since he lived in a penthouse nearby on Houston Street. Girls kept coming up to him, gushing, "I love your songs! Can I have your autograph?"

I looked at him quizzically.

He asked, "Don't you know who I am?" then said, "I'm Mike Black."

"I'm Rebecca Kade," I replied quizzically.

He said he was the lead singer of a rock band. I said, "Who are they?" He sang what I later realized was one of his hits, and added, "I'm kind of a big deal. People know who I am." He actually said that. It was pitiful. Or hilarious. I was working at the Comic Strip comedy club at the time as an assistant to the owner, Lucien Hold. At the Comic Strip, Lucien had helped discover people like Jerry Seinfeld, Eddie Murphy, Chris Rock, and Adam Sandler. I went with Lucien to hang out backstage at *Saturday Night Live* and to go to the after parties. I met Darrell Hammond, Chevy Chase (rude), Jimmy Fallon (great), Colin Quinn (wonderful), Conan O'Brien, Steven Tyler—all the hosts and musicians, just to name a few.

Fame meant nothing to me. Character did. That's what I told Mike, and he seemed to be a bit more respectful after that. For a while, anyway. We started dating seriously. At least, that's what I thought! I hung out backstage at his shows, and he showered me with pricey but bohemian clothes and jewelry. I was leading the rock-chick life.

A few months into our relationship, I got pregnant. It was on St. Patrick's Day. We used protection, so I don't know what happened. That's why I tell my daughter she was meant to be.

merry christmas, baby

Mike's band had a concert in New York at an intimate venue. I wasn't supposed to go that night, but I showed up backstage to tell him the news. Lo and behold, there was another girl there. Somebody named Suzanne. I was already distraught, and now I was furious. Why wouldn't I think there would be another woman?

He pulled me into a dressing room and we sat on a bench.

"You have to get an abortion," he told me. "We'll have plenty of time for the rest of our lives to have children." Yeah, right. I ran out in tears and fled home in a cab.

I called my mother. She was not happy. "You will have to raise this child, Rebecca. I am not going to."

I called my sister. It was the first of many drama calls we would have over the next few years.

"You will have this baby," Bridget insisted.

I was scared. I was making just enough money to get me through living in New York as a young single woman. How was I going to raise a child? Clearly, Mike had made his choice, and I made my peace with that. I continued to spend time with him. He was extremely sweet to me, which I later realized was just a ploy to get me to do what he wanted. He was trying to make me believe that we would be together forever and that we would have plenty of opportunities to have children in the future.

Despite his pressure, I was going to prenatal visits. My ob-gyn might have sensed how much Mike didn't want this baby. The doctor said that no matter what I decided, he would do whatever I asked of him. So, one day, after nonstop pressure from Mike— after days of him telling me I was only twenty-one, that I had my whole life ahead of me, that we had our whole lives together in front of us—I broke down. He convinced me to have an abortion. He said there was still time. I called my ob-gyn and scheduled the "procedure."

Mike said that I was doing the right thing and that he would meet me there that morning. But that night I sat up in bed and I thought and thought. And it hit me: this decision was mine. I wanted this baby so much. He didn't. I loved this baby already, and I didn't need Mike. I would find a way to make it work, because I am strong and a fighter and this baby deserved the best.

I called my doctor late in the night. He was completely fine with the late-night call. Maybe I read into it, but I thought he was proud of me.

Mike called and called the next day, and called again after learning from my doctor's office that I had canceled the abortion. "It's OK," he said in one message he left. "We can reschedule." He just didn't get it. He probably couldn't believe I wasn't simply doing what he wanted me to do. I truly believe to this day that he hates me for it. Not because I didn't have the abortion, but because he couldn't control me.

My grandfather was turning eighty in August, and there was a family reunion planned in North Carolina. It was the same night that Mike and his band were appearing at a H.O.R.D.E. (Horizons of Rock Developing Everywhere) Festival in Charlotte, North Carolina. Nobody in the family knew I was pregnant. My mom and I hatched a plan where we'd have a big dinner party for my grandfather's birthday. I would go to the concert to get Mike and bring him to the house so we could announce the baby together. I wanted my family to meet him before the baby was born so they could see he wasn't such a bad guy. Apart from the abortion argument, I still thought he was a decent man at that time.

When the day came, I was sitting at dinner next to my grandfather when he suddenly got up and made a speech: "Today, I am very happy," he said, "because I finally get to say I'm having my first great-grandchild." My mother had told him. "Rebecca is expecting, and she'll be bringing her boyfriend and his bandmates to the house this evening so everyone can meet them."

My aunts looked shocked. No one knew what to say, since my grandfather, the family patriarch, had condoned this out-of-wedlock baby.

I called Mike and told him, "The cat's out of the bag."

He freaked out. He said, "Give me some time. I need a few more drinks."

"I'll come and get you in a little while," I said. "Leave your bandmates behind, because they're always either high or drunk or both."

But just as I was about to leave, I couldn't believe what I saw out the window. Mike's tour bus was pulling up in front of the house.

My family is superconservative. The ladies cover themselves when they dress, and act like true Southern women. Just imagine the looks on their faces when Mike walked in with his long hair, looking like Jesus. Thankfully, his bandmates stayed on the bus. I didn't invite them in.

To my surprise, my grandfather stood up and shook Mike's hand when he walked in the door. He said, "Welcome to our family. We're very proud you're going to be a member of it. Thank you for bringing my great-grandchild into the world. I'm sure the rest of the family will welcome you." I was so proud of my grandfather at that moment. I always used to say to him, "Paw Paw, if I ever get married, it's going to have to be someone that is just like you." If only.

I'm sure my grandfather expected Mike to do the right thing and ask me to marry him. I tried to explain in the years that followed why it was better that we never did get married.

•   •   •

And then Mike suddenly left the country on tour. He didn't even tell me. He simply disappeared for months while I was pregnant. It was a harbinger of things to come: he was not going to be around a lot.

One day there was a message on my answering machine. It was him. He was back, he said, and he wanted to meet.

He came over. One of the places he had been to was Japan. He handed me a box. Inside was a little baby-blue kimono. He said, "This is my peace offering. If you will allow me to be part of having this baby, however you would like me to, I would like that to happen."

Soon it became evident that his contributions would be as tiny as that kimono. He wasn't talking about marrying me, or even living with me.

Our baby would need a crib, a stroller, clothing, and blankets. I'd gotten fired from my job for being pregnant, because I was always sick. Mike wasn't really talking about taking on the financial responsibilities of fatherhood. He was a guy who had been made rich by rock and was living in a penthouse in SoHo. All Mike was really talking about was showing up at a few Lamaze classes.

I was on my own, but then, my sister and I had been fending for ourselves since I was thirteen years old and she was fourteen. I would figure this out.

I got another job right away, at Fox Broadcasting. It paid me only $34,000 a year, but at least it had benefits. I would be covered for prenatal visits and the birth itself, especially if there were any complications during the delivery.

Mike did go to the doctor's appointments when he was in town. He went to the sonograms. But that was it. At thirty-one, he had not matured. He tried to grow up and act the way he thought a father should, but he was scared to death.

Our beautiful baby daughter was born in early December. On Christmas Eve, three weeks later, Mike came over. While I held our infant in my arms, he presented me with this news:

He said he really didn't know how to handle a child. He said, "I think I'll be a better dad once she can talk." He said, "I need someone who can have conversations." He was used to someone cleaning up after him, he said. So how was he going to look after a baby when he couldn't look after himself? He actually described the image of himself holding the baby in one arm and pushing the vacuum in the other and said he just didn't see himself doing that.

But that wasn't all.

"Rebecca," he said, "you're actually the 'other girl' in my life. I've been dating somebody else for two and a half years. She lives in Houston. She's a stripper. I'm going to marry her. We are working on moving her up here, and we're looking at houses."

Merry Christmas.

the worst happens

Mike actually insisted on taking a paternity test. I said, "Knock yourself out; I know you're Isabella's father." So did science. The lab results from Mike's DNA test came back 99.999 percent positive that he was her dad. It remained to be seen whether he could be a good one.

She lived with me, and he paid child support, but I supported her by working full-time at Viacom in the Internal Audit department. And I prayed.

Going to a Baptist church four days a week when I was growing up did have an impact on me, and not always a good one. I haven't attended as regularly since I was given freedom.

However, I was and still am a believer. I felt like God and I had a pretty good connection through prayer directly, but there were times when I felt lost and empty, and for some reason going to church with a congregation made me feel better. Now that Isabella was getting older, I sought out a church and found one I liked—but it was Catholic. I had had an aunt and uncle who were Catholic, and when I had stayed with them in Tennessee they brought me to Mass. At this Catholic church in New York, I was given the opportunity to be absolved each week if I truly repented and accepted Christ, instead of being yelled at for my sins when I was asking for forgiveness. I enjoyed Communion. I studied the catechism by going to night classes twice a week and seriously considered converting to become a full practicing Catholic. Living in New York, I thought it would feel so special to have that conversion ceremony take place in St. Patrick's Cathedral. I attended the Church of the Blessed Sacrament regularly, and during the Christmas season I volunteered my time to help with the holiday decorations. It made me feel closer to God, and I also felt it was a way to repent for my sins.

For the first six years of Isabella's life, I raised her almost entirely on my own. I rarely used babysitters, because I felt guilty enough about having to work during the day. My good friend Hana was Isabella's caretaker as a baby when I first went back to work. It was the only reason I felt OK about being away. She loved Isabella even before she was born. My daughter was a mama's girl. At one point we had a garden apartment on the Upper West Side, so we worked in our garden and tended our beautiful hydrangeas with care. She loved it. I got her a pool that was big enough for her to swim around in to cool off in the summer, and we would cook on the grill and sit out under the gazebo that we put up in the back and wrapped in white Christmas lights. At night it was our private, twinkling oasis. Isabella's favorite thing to do was read, and she would ask me to read stories over and over and over again, never getting tired of them. It was only when she fell fast asleep that we would stop. Before she was taken from my home, when I left work each evening, all I could think about was getting back to my little girl.

One morning a few months shy of Isabella's seventh birthday, Mike called up and said, "My dad's flying in tomorrow morning. I was wondering if I could take Isabella to breakfast with him." I thought the rare visit with her grandfather would be good for Isabella. "Sure," I said.

"Also, I got tickets for *Beauty and the Beast* tonight," he added. "Can I take her to *Beauty and the Beast*? That way I'll have her till tomorrow morning." I said, "Of course."

I put Isabella in a beautiful dress and shoes and gave her a little sleepover bag with her pj's and toothbrush in it.

"Have fun, bunny!" I said with a hug as a friend of his picked her up. That's when I should have known something was wrong. He couldn't even face me, knowing what he was about to do.

I was glad for her that night, and after work the next day was anxious to hear how she had enjoyed it. Mike was supposed to bring her back by six o'clock. When I didn't hear from him by seven, I became concerned and called him. I called and called his cell; I called his landline. There was no response.

At first I feared the worst: that a stranger had somehow gotten hold of her and taken her. But Mike's silence was mystifying.

I jumped into a taxi and went over to his building. He didn't have a doorman, so I buzzed his apartment for what seemed like hours. Again no response. That's when I realized it was Mike who had taken my daughter. I started sobbing right there in the lobby.

It was all premeditated. Mike had planned the kidnapping days in advance, creating the ruse of a visit with her grandfather and a Broadway show.

I went back to my apartment and called the police. I reported that my daughter had been kidnapped by her father. I wanted them to go over and just get her. But they said the only thing they could do was to file a warrant for his arrest and an order for him to produce Isabella in court.

I wasn't certain where my child was for eleven days. Mike wouldn't answer me. The police couldn't help me. Was she with him? Was she distraught and begging to go home? How would she sleep without her favorite things? Without me reading to her from her children's Bible? How would she fall asleep without our lullaby that we sang together each night?

I felt as if I was going absolutely out of my mind. Mike was ten steps ahead of me. He'd gotten lawyered up and had filed in family court for temporary full custody of the child to whom he'd only occasionally paid attention for six years.

In New York, if a person tells the court they believe it is in the best interest of the child, the court gives the child to them, whether the claim is true or false, until a hearing can be held. I simply had no choice but to wait for my day in court. The court informed me that at some point I would be served papers detailing the accusations Mike had made to win that temporary order. Again I waited for those papers so I could know what I was up against. Why was I such a terrible mother that he tore Isabella away from me?

Mike kept Isabella for weeks without letting me see her.

The only thing he would tell me was that she was physically safe.

I continued to go work in the Financial District every day, going through the motions like an automaton, and each night I would go into Isabella's room and lie on her bed and pray. I prayed that God would somehow send her my love and that she would be able to feel it, wherever she was. I thought about all of those people out there who had missing loved ones; I honestly do not know how they get through an entire hour, much less a day. I was devastated. How could it be? How could this possibly be real? I was so worried about Isabella. I was worried about what she was thinking and how she was feeling. Was she scared? What was he telling her? How was he explaining to her that she could not see the one person on whom she had most counted in her life: her mother?

I showed up to the family court building on Lafayette Street. It was the first time I had seen Mike since he took Isabella. I don't think there will ever be words to describe the emotion I felt that day. I felt so small, yet my rage was bigger than that building. I thought for sure, as soon as we got in front of a judge, Mike's claim would all be dismissed. The judge told me that Mike was taking Isabella away from me. Just like that. Mike told me, "You will never have her again."

Oh, yes I will, I thought. *You don't know who you're messing with.* I realized I had to get a new lawyer—the best in the business—but how was I going to pay for it?

Mike had his wife's best friend testify that I popped Vicodin and left pills around the house while the friend babysat for me once. I was speechless: How was I supposed to defend myself in front of a person who would say these things in court despite hardly knowing me?

Mike also maintained that an old friend I had in the house was a danger to Isabella. The judge told me that she wouldn't entertain my request for custody "until you are no longer in a position where your current paramour is living with you."

That "current paramour" wasn't a lover at all. When the custody hearing began in August 2005, I had an old friend—I'll call him Bruce—who had been convicted of and served time for a terrible assault on a woman. He'd served his time and now had nowhere to go. I pitied him. He told me he hadn't committed the crime, and I believed him. I let him stay with us till he got on his feet. Clearly, this was not my smartest move in life. And I do regret it.

Later, one of Mike's exes confided to me that what he really wanted was to stop having to pay me child support. It would be easier on his wallet if his new wife looked after Isabella, supplemented by a cheap nanny who ultimately ended up watching Isabella most of the time, as he was always out nights or away on tour. I do in fact believe that not having to pay child support was Mike's real motivation for going to court, because I did immediately oust Bruce from my house—he was out of there within forty-eight hours—yet Mike still pursued full custody.

One day, in among the bills in my mailbox was a square envelope with a child's lettering on the front: it was Isabella's writing. Inside was a picture she drew of herself crying. Across the top were the words "Mommy, come get me!" There would be more; somehow, the nanny was willing to secretly mail them to me.

Even Mike had to see how miserable she was. He decided I could see her, but what he did next—or what his lawyer convinced the judge to do—was incredibly cruel. They allowed me to see Isabella, but only on supervised visits. I actually had to pay someone to chaperone me as I spent time with my own daughter. She sat near us and listened to every word. This would happen in our own home or in the park—I had to get her permission to take my own daughter to the park! It was ridiculous and demeaning. Isabella was so young; she didn't know why this third person was there. She just knew she was coming home to be with her mother and her beloved dog, Sally.

They would allow me only two-hour visits twice a week. Isabella and I had to make every single second count. Even getting to and from her dad's place took time. So we'd sing in the cab. We'd do a lot of baking. I gave her a lot of books. Reading was still one of her favorite things to do. She was just happy to curl up with a book and Sally at her feet.

But then it would be time for her to go, and the supervisor would take her from me. These were heartbreaking moments, but I tried to be strong and cheerful for Isabella.

Eventually, Mike decided it was in Isabella's interest to give me more time with her. I got to have her every other weekend and on Wednesdays for dinner.

Even then, the visits had to be overseen by someone we knew. If I took Isabella to a restaurant, her father would have to be sitting at a table nearby—not with us but with his wife or a friend, listening in on our conversations. It was absolutely humiliating, and all about control.

Mike was always claiming that I was being too emotional with Isabella. How could I not be emotional when I missed her so much? After a while I learned to become stoic. I would then go home and hyperventilate, trying in vain to quell my anxiety. I'd breathe in and out of a paper bag. It just hurt so badly. I began to wonder if this was what my life—what Isabella's life—was going to be like until she was grown. I understand that children are resilient, but she was deeply unhappy.

The judge ordered all of us to have a forensic psychiatric evaluation. This is common in family court: an objective party evaluates family members individually, then observes how a child interacts with her mother, her father, and anyone else who would be in her life on a daily basis. Mike had married hurriedly, right before he filed for custody. Within a year the marriage was over. He was gone most of the time, and Isabella was left with nannies overnight. Surely the judge would see this for what it was and end this entire fiasco. Surely common sense would prevail.

In a thirty-page report, an independent forensic psychiatric evaluator concluded that Isabella preferred to be with her mother and did not seem to have a connection with her father. He recommended that the child be returned to me. The judge ruled that the report, from her handpicked evaluator, was not admissible and would remain sealed. No one was to receive a copy, and it could never leave the courtroom. I was floored. She actually said that the evaluator must have not understood his job. I knew right then that I was screwed and that this was a setup. I was going to go out and get so much money that I would be able to fight this all the way to the Supreme Court if I had to.

incalls and outcalls

The huge legal bills appearing in my mailbox terrified me, so I worked for Kristin whenever I could. Isabella wasn't allowed to be at my apartment, so that made it easy for me to work for Kristin. For a while I was working at my day job until five, and then at night I'd work for Kristin until four or five in the morning. Then I'd get a couple of hours' sleep and get to the office by eight thirty a.m. The next day I'd do it all over again. Court appearances had started to eat up my vacation days, and I was on thin ice at work.

I was very tired, and my work during the day suffered. Finally my boss fired me. But by then I was making so much money at Kristin's that it more than made up for that paycheck. The money was far better than anything else available to a girl who had not finished college, but still, Kristin took half of everything I earned. And beauty costs money: I had to make sure my hair was always touched up at the roots, that I was tanned and manicured and waxed properly, that my clothes were pressed. It was expensive, but I was able to pay rent and the ever-looming legal bills.

From Kristin I learned how the escort business worked. She had me doing both incalls and outcalls. With incalls we worked at the madam's locations—the media revels in calling them brothels—and we literally worked eight-hour shifts, like secretaries and cashiers do. It's typically at least a two-bedroom apartment, and there is usually another girl there with you for company and some security. The madam has a booker, who is careful to stagger the appointments so that clients who do business together or are in the same social circle are spared the embarrassment of bumping into one another coming or going, or in the event that they want to take a shower.

When you are on incall, you are expected to stay in the apartment the entire shift without leaving, to calm the suspicions of the neighbors. Chances are their eyebrows are already raised by the gentlemen coming and going at all hours, not to mention the loud moans and shouts of orgasm and the sound of headboards knocking against the walls. Kristin just asked us to keep it down as much as possible to reduce the risk for all of us. You can see how well that worked.

Incall is like a factory: you work as much as you can, and see as many people as you can. The price per hour is lower, but you can make thousands and thousands of dollars in one day without ever leaving the apartment. Kristin's apartment at the

Corinthian was a two-bedroom, so she could have two clients in at a time. There would usually be two girls there, and sometimes other girls would stop by to chat and keep the others company. It also provided a bit of security, especially at night. There was no security man or bodyguard at all. If some big guy got rough, you were out of luck. I did the same for the others. We'd sit in the living room and chat until the client arrived.

I did more outcalls, where I went to the client. Outcall can be either to the client's home, a hotel room, or even to a yacht or a private jet. In town, we might meet at a bar and go out to dinner, a party, or a concert. The money is much more per hour, and—depending on the girl and how she is ranked by the madam on sex-for-sale websites like eros-ny.com and backpage.com—a girl can make a lot doing very little and actually have a great time. Outcalls were expected to be stretched out as long as possible because they are hundreds more per hour.

When I met a client at a hotel, the only security I had was the phone call Kristin would make to ask the front desk for the guest in his stated room number to see if he was really who he said he was. It could have been Jack the Ripper posing as John Doe for all I knew.

I quickly learned how to be discreet in upscale hotels like the Waldorf Astoria and the Pierre. Going to these places in the beginning, I felt it was obvious who I was and what I was doing there. I'm sure the doormen and concierge in particular saw us coming a mile away. In my five-inch Jimmy Choo stilettos and form-fitting Marc Jacobs sheath, it was clear I wasn't a delegate to the actuaries convention. I didn't look like a hooker, but usually a woman dressed that alluringly does not come back to her hotel room alone.

Discretion was crucial for me, so I decided that the best approach was not to duck and run but rather to engage with them and look them straight in the eye with a "Good evening." I always wanted to look assured and as if I knew where I was going, even if I had no clue where the elevators were. It was all about projecting confidence, pretending that I belonged in that world.

Upon arriving at the client's room, I'd introduce myself with my nom de guerre. Kristin had told me not to give my real name and not to ask theirs, but most of the time they'd give their real name anyway. If they were famous, obviously I'd recognize them. And I'd hope that, whatever the booker told the client, I was playing the right part.

We all had to give Kristin a schedule, which gave windows of when we would be available to be called at a moment's notice. I might get a text saying *Be at the Waldorf in 20 minutes* and I'd have to be ready.

And just because you did your job, it didn't mean you were done for the night. You could be called to do another. Outcall money was amazing if we were on the good side of the booker, Lucy, or Kristin herself.

As a high-priced call girl, it actually helps to be a decent conversationalist. These are sophisticated men. They don't want bimbos. There are some men who want the bimbo type, but they are not willing to pay big money for it. Yes, they want sex, but they don't want to feel as if they are slumming it. They want companionship. If you follow what's happening in the world and are cultured, well, the sky's the limit.

Why do these men pay so much for sex? The short answer is that they want a woman who will do things sexually that their wives aren't doing. Some want things like bondage or rougher sex but are afraid to ask their wives.

But the wives of these men aren't doing something else that is the relationship killer: making them feel special. This was a common complaint. I tried to make men feel that there was nothing more important to me at that moment than what they were saying. *They work hard,* I told myself. *They deserve it.* I've learned a tremendous amount about the economy, investing, politics, and the law from my clients. These are the men who were raised to rule, or who got on top of their industry by sheer brains and determination. The only other way I would have met men at this level would have been if I were a CEO myself. And, yes, I'll admit that I was aware that the attention I paid them paid me back in spades. More than once I counted the cash I was given twice because I couldn't believe how huge the "tip" was. Sometimes it was more than the fee. And Kristin didn't get a cut of that.

Also, men love a fresh face, and when you are the new girl, you make a ton of money.

When business in New York was good, Kristin would make forays into other territories, and she'd have the girls test out different markets. She had already set up the Philadelphia site, but we went to Boston and Washington, D.C., for her. We'd go from city to city, and clients would get an online "lookbook" so they could choose which girls they wanted and when.

It's amazing how each city has its own sexual vibe. New York has so many high flyers in finance, entertainment, and the media, many of whom have built themselves up from humble origins. They're men who've had to make a lot of hard decisions in life in order to get where they are, and although many have an air of entitlement, they seemed to respect and appreciate us. It was in New York where we also had our encounters with visitors: European aristocrats, Asian billionaires, Middle Eastern royalty.

But in Philadelphia, where Kristin kept an apartment at 1600 Walnut Street, within walking distance of Rittenhouse Square Park, our clients were more down to earth. Conversations flowed more easily. Clients were mostly from the real estate and finance world, but they did not have the New York arrogance. They even dressed more casually. Sometimes I questioned whether they could afford me. In Philly a man will linger over a beer with a girl and talk sports. It was refreshing. Same with Boston: Boston men are "chill"—and absolute sports fanatics. Wear a Red Sox cap and a thong, and they go crazy.

I had one regular client in Philly who was engaged to a doctor. Her schedule made for a very difficult personal life for him sexually, so I was merely a release or retreat from the frustration that he would have for the rest of his life, should he go through with his marriage to her. Another regular client there was one of the biggest Republicans in Pennsylvania. Kristin would have his favorite girl, whose pseudonym was Rowan, come up from Florida for him.

The men in Washington were insane. It was a company town, and power was the product. They had a whole other concept of what prostitution was. There were some threesomes, which was fine. But they wouldn't leave after their appointed time. And everybody in D.C. was expecting bare backing. No condoms. Who on earth would take that chance? They were abusive, mean, and relentless. The first time I went to Washington, I was supposed to stay for five days; I left after two. We did not do any further market research in D.C. after that. Kristin sent me back to another state's capital, and that's where I had sex with my first governor.

two governors

traveled to a certain city and checked into an apartment that Kristin maintained there. I was supposed to meet a man named Trevor. He wouldn't be hard to miss: He drove an Aston Martin—James Bond's vehicle of choice—and when the silver, aerodynamic work of art whirred up to the curb, I stepped right in.

Trevor was handsome. No: he was drop-dead gorgeous, and he seemed pleasant enough in the short time it took for him to drive me a couple of blocks to a restaurant. We could have walked, but I never question clients! It was a lovely space, with French doors opening onto a small park. It was early spring, and crocuses had popped up around each tree. I chuckled to myself at the phallic imagery.

Trevor and I were having a cocktail at the bar, when he turned to me and nodded.

"That's our governor over there having lunch with some of my friends," he said. "Would you like to meet him?"

"That depends on if he's a liberal or not," I joked. "I'm a Republican, you know."

He chuckled, took me by the hand, led me over to the governor's table, and introduced me as Ashley.

"Governor, I don't know if you should be seen with these reprobates," Trevor ventured, causing his pals to laugh. "I'd like you to meet Ashley . . . Smith. Watch it: she's a fiscal conservative."

"Well, she's a hell of a lot prettier than Jan Brewer," he guffawed. "Nice to meet you, Ashley."

He should have said "Ashleys." I could have sworn the governor said that right to my breasts.

Other than that, he was really gracious. It was casual. I shook his hand, and Trevor and I returned to the bar. I didn't think much of it. But I thought it was weird that Trevor would take someone whom he'd hired to meet the governor. Trevor said the governor was a client of his. It could have been true.

We stayed at the bar, talking for two hours about politics, why I was in this business, and what I was really going to do with my life. He really wanted to know, and he had a way of making you want to tell him. I told him nothing about Isabella, but at this point I had gone back to school, and that was an easy topic to bring up and discuss with any client. We finished our drinks and then drove back to the apartment. Trevor came up and we had sex. For such a great-looking guy, I guess any girl would be hopeful that he would have been absolutely amazing. And he was, but it wasn't that blow-me-out-of-the-water sex that he should have reciprocated. It was fine, though. In this business, you get used to that.

I was still in town a couple of days later when Kristin's booker called. She told me that Trevor wanted another "date." Frankly, that perplexed me. Trevor was a very young guy, handsome enough to be an actor. He was single, impeccably dressed, manicured in every way. He was extremely confident, and he appeared to have money. This was a man who would have no problem getting girls. Based on how things went last time, it must have been a lot better for him than it was for me. Check for my ego.

Trevor said he wanted to come directly to the apartment this time. When he arrived, he rang the doorbell and I buzzed him through. I opened the door, and to my surprise, it was not Trevor standing there. It was the governor, smiling. For a split second I thought he was in the wrong place, but I recovered in a beat and invited him in. *Ah, now I get it*, I thought. Trevor was literally test driving me for his boss.

The governor was in no hurry. He strolled over to the sofa and sat down. He was more than pleasant. He wasn't chatty, but he did ask me about myself, and I said I was a student. My clients always liked that I was in college. There was no strangeness whatsoever between us, but I did keep expecting him to acknowledge that we had met previously at the restaurant through Trevor. He never brought it, or Trevor, up. He had the situation under complete control.

Still, I sensed a neediness about him. Because he was a governor, I hesitated to touch him. But he soon made the first move, and there it all began. He was "old-school": no foreplay, just enough action to get him hard enough to perform. Although he would try to be a man and take charge, he wasn't exactly going to finish that way, so I always had to take control. And he never talked during sex, but afterward it was clear that he wanted to feel like he had blown my socks off. He'd grin from ear to ear, and from the way he looked at me, I got the feeling he believed I really wanted him.

He was a member of the good old boys' club, if there really is such a thing. The kind of powerful man who would sit in a room somewhere smoking a cigar and talking smugly—and with plenty of exaggeration—about what he had just done to me. I think he bought into the idea that I was impressed with power. Little did he know that "governor" ranked pretty low on my client list.

He didn't even take an hour. I never questioned him when he left without paying. I was sure he wouldn't, forgive the pun, screw me over, and that I would be hearing from Trevor. After all, I certainly had something on the married governor now, didn't I?

I saw the governor several times over the next year or so. I never met him in public, of course. He always came to the apartment. Always at night, around dinnertime. On all the dates, no money ever exchanged hands between us. Trevor handled the money.

I never had a problem with him, unlike another governor I had as a client. He was never chatty. But you could tell he genuinely needed the affection he apparently wasn't getting at home. He was very appreciative. Someone who appreciated you taking time with him. He never tried to give you the feeling that you were lucky to have him as a client. I'm not saying it was a girlfriend relationship, but the sex was very relaxed, calm, and pleasurable. Nothing freaky. And he would always say thank you.

Still, I thought of my sister and my political friends from the other side of the aisle. Oh, what they could have done with that tidbit of information. *He'd better watch it,* I thought. I hoped he wasn't so free with others who might start talking.

Oh, but he was an angel compared to another governor I had as a client. As the whole world knows by now, New York governor Eliot Spitzer was a client of Kristin's. They heard about Ashley Dupré. They didn't hear about me.

It was an appointment set up two or three days in advance. It wasn't one of those Can-you-be-somewhere-in-an-hour? things. Kristin said it was an important client, but she didn't say who. She briefed me on what he liked—what he expected. He needed the scenario specified to the girl in advance. He's a role-play kind of guy.

He didn't want mainstream intercourse. He definitely wanted a struggle.

There was a whole dialogue I was supposed to have with him. I was supposed to say I had just been to a self-defense class. He was supposed to respond: "Well, then, let's see if you learned anything. Can you protect yourself?" He would be the aggressor. I would have to defend myself.

I was at Kristin's apartment at the Corinthian in the middle of the afternoon. Kristin was working on her computer in the other room when he arrived.

Ah, I thought when I answered the door, *this is the reason for all the secrecy and preparation.* Why didn't Kristin just tell me? Did she think I wouldn't recognize him?

He had his jacket off. He was in a shirt and tie. He was

cordial enough, but there was no suggestion that we have a drink together. There was none of that.

He said he didn't want to wear a condom. I said that was not negotiable.

He then started to feel out whether I understood what was expected: that I was supposed to show him some of the things I'd learned in my "self-defense" class, and then he would show me a thing or two. I told him I understood.

He just jumped right in. He was like some of the guys who envision themselves in a porn movie. No initial tenderness at all.

It was really about pretending it was a struggle. He wanted to believe that the situation was real, that he was attacking me and that I was defending myself. He put up a pretty good fight.

It was I who was taking control of him initially. I felt really stupid at first. But then I got it. I'm pretty strong. I think he was gauging my strength.

I didn't feel I was acting after a while. He preferred it. The more struggle there was, the more he was into it. He became extremely comfortable with what was happening. You can tell when someone finds a comfort zone. He was so into the situation. Now this girl understands; here we go.

I remember holding his wrists, him pushing back, me trying to hold my stance, and then we moved to the bed. My clothes came off in the fray.

He really wanted to be in control. It was all about restraint and holding me down until I was nearly helpless. He really put on a lot of pressure, pinning me to the bed. That didn't bother me. That's what I was told to expect.

It takes a lot to scare me. I've been through a lot. But at this point I was starting to get worried.

He wasn't pretending to be a rapist. But he was like an attacker.

I still had my lingerie on. He was naked. He was aroused. I thought, *What can I do to get this part over with? What can I do? At some point we have to get down to having sex and move on.*

I remember trying to push myself up off the bed. That made him apply more pressure. It happened so quickly. I think when I pushed up, he thought I was asking for more. He applied more force. Almost the entire time was consumed with this struggle.

It wasn't that easy to get out from under him. This wasn't playtime. He was taking it really seriously. He was getting what he wanted. He liked the struggle. There was no safety code word we'd agreed upon. I hadn't thought it would get this intense. *He doesn't know I'm being serious that enough is enough,* I thought. I was really worried. It got rough. And then he put his hands around my throat, strangling me.

When he grabbed my throat, that was too much. He wasn't squeezing. He was pushing down. I was on my back. I don't know if he was trying to really hurt me, but he was.

He took it a little too far. Maybe if I were more experienced, which I was not, it would have gone on. I was nervous. I was worried. *This is not OK,* I thought.

After it was over, he got dressed to go. He never said, "I'm sorry, are you OK?" Nothing of the kind. He acted like everything was normal. But before he left, he gave me a very big tip. It was separate from the pay, which was about $1,500 an hour, and Kristin was going to handle that. Maybe it was to keep me from saying something. Or maybe he was sorry. I do remember him perspiring a lot. My friend who knows a little Yiddish calls him "Governor Schvitzer."

the last great madam: anna gristina

Kristin was too flamboyant, and she was becoming too unpredictable. When she got drunk, she'd pitch hissy fits and do things like throw her phone against the wall. The longer I worked for her, the more convinced I became that she would get busted.

The job had become less and less outcall, which meant less money in my pocket and an even bigger hit to my soul. I felt like I was becoming less and less of Rebecca, and I didn't know who I was. Things were not going well in court; money was not coming in; and my heart and love of my life, my daughter, Isabella, was still not back home with me. I was working eight-hour shifts at

Kristin's apartment, and I felt like I was going to a job. I couldn't believe I had gotten to the point where I had accepted that *this* was my job. It was depressing. I was lying to everyone about how I was making money, and it was getting really hard to keep up with who I told what. I'd go home after a long day of incall work and Kristin or her booker, Lucy, might suddenly call and ask me to go back out on an outcall.

One night Kristin sent me on an outcall to a client's apartment. We went to clients' apartments all the time, passing photographs of their wives and children in silver frames on the grand piano on the way to the master bedroom.

This client was a major New York real estate developer. He liked to wear women's underwear, so we called him Panty Man. He had a whole case of silk panties, albeit very large panties, in his apartment. There was a lot of hush-hush about it. Kristin didn't want a lot of discussion because she was afraid that new girls wouldn't want to go. He was one of Kristin's regulars and paid by credit card.

I went to his apartment on the Upper East Side. He answered the door in a thong. He was a very overweight man, and his stomach was in rolls. You couldn't see the thong at first. He looked to be in his forties.

His apartment was huge and beautifully decorated, but that night it was in disarray. Perhaps his wife had taken the kids for a ski vacation; who knows? He had video cameras mounted all over the place. We passed his teenage daughter's bedroom; it was immaculate, like a neat little fortress against the weirdness.

He then brought out the cocaine. He did so much blow. He asked me if I wanted some, and didn't mind when I said no. Some clients do.

He asked me to use sex toys—on him. He wanted it to go on for hours, but I just said I couldn't extend the session because I had another appointment. I think it was the thong.

The job just seemed to be getting worse and worse. I worked briefly for a different agency that operated like a factory. It was ridiculous. They wanted me to rent my own hotel room and have sex with as many guys as possible, all day long. I made $6,000 or $7,000 in a day. It was a time when I really needed cash to get up-to-date with my bills, especially for Ms. Alter. I did it for about ten days straight. I made a lot of money, but my body was completely torn apart and exhausted. I was a mess, physically and mentally.

Another escort at Kristin's, Olivia, told me she secretly worked for another madam. She didn't want Kristin to know. But her competitor had operated totally under the radar for fifteen years in New York City, with business around the world. She had the most beautiful girls flying in from around the country, and the wealthiest clients would book them in advance like a celebrity junket. Olivia bragged about how much money she was making with this other madam. I said, "*Please* give me her number."

I called her the very next day and explained my situation. The woman had an accent; was it Irish? No, Scottish. She called herself Caroline. Only later would I learn that I had been speaking to the legendary Anna Scotland. Aka Anna Tennant. Aka Anna Gristina.

She replied, "I have to have you checked out. I don't take just anyone. Go to this address. My friend Christie will meet with you there."

Olivia had told me that nobody gets to meet "Caroline" directly. A lot of girls never saw her face. Neither did most of her clients. Most people had no idea what she looked like. And the truth was that Olivia had only done one job for Anna, and it had been a specialty job. She wasn't working for her as a girl on her roster. Anna was confused about how I got her number in the first place and was nervous about it, so I revealed my source. Anna proclaimed, "Well, then, she'll never work for me again." Pretty harsh, and I got the message. I passed that number to no one.

I went to the predetermined place, and Anna's intermediary, Christie, was there waiting for me. I met her at a well-appointed apartment on the Upper East Side for a meet-and-greet. I had to sit and talk for a while. She wanted to know everything about me. I was pretty forthcoming about who I had worked for before and why I was moving on. I talked about how I grew up and where I came from. She also asked me what films I liked, whether I'd read any good books lately. What restaurants I went to. I think she was trying to determine whether I could hold an intelligent conversation with cultured men.

Then she asked me to undress completely. I'm slender, with natural breasts and a slim waist. I have long legs, and no cellulite, thanks to years at the gym. My hair is naturally pale blond, and it's down to my hips.

Christie walked around me, and when we were face-to-face, she reacted with one word: "Great!" Christie asked if I was ready to work. "Oh, I'm ready, all right," I answered.

"Then you're going to have to leave Kristin Davis and not say where you're going," she said. "Caroline expects exclusivity." This was actually the first time I had ever heard someone ask anyone to do that. But I liked it. It made me feel like this was on an entirely different level. That would be an understatement. I had no idea what I was about to get myself into.

After my first job for Anna, I had no problem with that. The client paid me $5,000, and my cut was $3,500. Anna's clients paid more and tipped way better—they might leave a four-figure tip—and because Anna had had clients herself at one time, she gave the girls 60 percent, unlike Kristin's half cut. I said to myself, *OK! If this is what this woman can deliver, I'm in.*

Soon after, Christie called to find out my availability for a photo shoot with a well-known photographer who has a secret side business photographing call girls. Anna had rented out a house, hired a caterer, and organized a couple dozen of the sixty or so women she had working for her at the time to pose. It was a snow scene, and we wore elf hats and furry boots and, well, little else. She also had us pose for the clients' lookbook. She kept all of our photos so we couldn't bring them to another agency. This was entirely new for me. I had never had photos taken. This meant that clients would actually see the real me when they were deciding which girl to book.

Kristin used to do a bait-and-switch where she'd lure clients with photos of super-hot girls on her website. I don't know how many of them actually worked for her. Anna wanted nude pictures, but not raunchy *Hustler* magazine–type shots. She wanted sensual, tasteful photography. She liked it if you could pull the *Playboy* look. She wanted you to be enticing and playful but not show everything. You were supposed to be a gift-wrapped present that someone would want to open up. That all sounded good. But posing for her photographer, Robert, was excruciating. Because of my Baptist past, I was never comfortable getting naked for a camera. But Robert told me to think about one man I cared about. That actually worked, and I relaxed.

I had the most fun at the shoots that were the theme concepts. Anna would splurge for the best costumes to be custom-made, and for the best hair and makeup stylists to prep us. We'd do holiday shoots for Christmas, Hanukkah, Valentine's Day, and St. Patrick's Day. The Christmas and Hanukkah hooker photographs could become collectors' items, if Anna or Robert would ever release them.

Anna also had us shoot fantasy scenes. She'd appeal to guys who were coming in for Super Bowl weekend by having a few of us girls dress up in tiny football jerseys and helmets and little else. We did one girl-on-girl shoot dressed as schoolgirls. Nothing hard-core. It just let customers know that they could have two girls at once if they wished.

Anna Gristina will probably come to be known as the last great New York madam before prostitution is legalized. She presented the sexiest, most sophisticated young women in the business—women you would never suspect of being escorts—to the wealthiest, most powerful men. And she used the most discreet, high-tech methods available to keep it all completely under the radar of law enforcement for nearly fifteen years.

Anna kept a small apartment on East Seventy-Eighth Street for occasional encounters in the afternoon, and for the girls to drop off and pick up payments. Only a few knew where she hid the bulk of the money inside. There was a safe bolted to the floor inside one of the closets in the very back. It was well hidden; unless you were looking for it, you would totally miss it. I still have a set of keys. But I mostly met men on their own chosen turf, wherever in the world that might be.

Anna served clients from all over the world: London. Tokyo. Paris. Barcelona. Several cities in Italy. The former Soviet Union. Switzerland. The Middle East. In the States, LA, Vegas, Washington, D.C., Miami, Philadelphia, Boston, and of course, New York. And she got the most beautiful girls in the country to fly in.

I could make $25,000, plus expenses, for a weekend date abroad. Even though I'd only work for maybe two hours. I'd spend more time just getting there.

Anna's clients were people who had *real* money. It was a network that operated by word of mouth, for the most part. The clients tended to be in their forties and fifties, and they were at the top of their game, with plenty of money to spare. Some of them were responsible for the 2008 Wall Street crisis. They were bankers, luxury-brand CEOs, celebrity restaurateurs, club owners, hedge fund managers, producers, musicians—men with significant wealth. Some had private jets; some had yachts. They might have a house in Aspen or Telluride; many had major homes in the Hamptons and ran in the same set. They didn't care if your picture was taken with them. They would always have an explanation for anybody who had a question. Society photographer Patrick McMullan took my photo with a married client who sits on several prestigious boards.

Anna's clients used their real names. Their executive assistants often made my travel arrangements on their credit cards. I hated that, because then the line was crossed. I never wanted anyone to know my real name. But with serious travel like first-class tickets to Asia or suites at the Conrad Tokyo, yes, you bet my name had to be on the bill; but so did theirs, so we both had insurance as far as I was concerned. I didn't want them to screw with my personal life, but then, they didn't want me to screw with theirs, either. We had an understanding.

Anna's clients didn't want girls whose appearance screamed, "Hooker!" They don't want a quick fix from a Barbie who can't handle a conversation with their friends. Anna's girls were totally different from anybody else's.

She flew a lot of women in from other states. There was always a rotation. It wasn't the same girls all the time. These were the sexiest, most beautiful girls in the business, and that was the reputation Anna had. As for the girls who lived in New York, the only way she took you on was if someone told her you'd be a great fit. If she was interested, she might call you.

Unlike Kristin, Anna was extremely discreet. She rarely let anyone meet her. Most of the clients, and many of the girls, never saw her face until the trial. She didn't advertise, and she sent pictures of the girls only to clients who requested them. Her website was password protected, and you had to be a member who had been thoroughly researched and checked out. A lot of clients came to her by word of mouth from trusted longtime regulars.

She didn't keep an office in the United States. She claims to have had one in Montreal. All her mobile phones had Montreal area codes, since prostitution is legal in Canada. Anna had so many different phone numbers. Once I counted ten different numbers stored in my phone for her. No one person had all of them. The computers at her farm in upstate New York had software that could scrub her hard drive in an instant if she were to be arrested.

The only person Anna trusted as a booker was her own sister, whom she referred to as Elizabeth. Elizabeth was much older, and because Anna had told us that her mother had had her when she was sixteen years old, we wondered if Elizabeth was really her mother. Anna said she had been adopted as the seventh child of a poor gardener and his wife in Scotland. It seemed unusual for such a poor couple to take on that added responsibility. I believe she started out in the business very young, and Elizabeth came along for the ride. In any case, Elizabeth was the one who knew all Anna's secrets. Like where her money went.

Law enforcement had no idea who she was or where she was, and they had had no photo of her for at least ten years. Compared to Anna's operation, Kristin's was like clown school, according to the Manhattan DA's office.

When I finally met Anna Gristina, she was all decked out in a fur coat, with expensive highlights in her hair, and wearing good jewelry. She was married to a younger man named Kelvin Gorr. He is the one who got reprimanded by the judge for bringing their children to her trial. She once told me, "I make all the money."

Her older children, one of whom is in college, are by other fathers. She still had some sort of relationship with her sugar daddy, who had been her client for years and even after she was married gifted her with two Range Rovers: one silver, one green. You could say the escort business was very, very good to Anna Gristina. Until it got bad.

Unlike many of the girls, I was slowly allowed into Anna's world. She would let me know when she was coming into the city, even if it was with her kids, and we would hang out. I met her at Paragon Sports once and just chilled as the boys picked out hockey equipment. Yes, she really was a hockey mom.

Anna used to say to me that I wasn't like the other girls. She would tell me that she was proud of me and I was going to make something of my life. Whenever she said that, it was a strange feeling, because I felt she actually meant it. I was going to school. I wasn't the typical drugged-out drunk hooker; I was reliable and consistent, and she valued that.

I don't know if it was because of our increasing closeness, but Anna began to hook me up with bigger and bigger clients.

Here is one of the reviews of me that a client—a very successful artist who would fly in from California for our trysts—posted on The Erotic Review, the Yelp of the sex business:

It had been a long time since I had seen any provider, because I'd been so disappointed by the last couple of experiences, so I wanted to choose very carefully this time. Ashley seemed to be just what I was looking for, at least physically, but I usually stay away from agencies. But a fellow TER member assured me that this agency was different than all the others. Not only was he right about the agency (they were so helpful in accommodating my crazy schedule) but Ashley was just what I expected and something more.

I didn't expect to meet a woman who was so engaging and intelligent. This wasn't like going to see a professional in the sex business. It was more like going over to hang with a woman that I might have met in class. Ashley looked like the quintessential blonde California college girl; barefoot and in comfortably worn jeans and a tank top that showed just enough of her smooth flat stomach to whet my sexual appetite. Eventually, we got into a discussion of existential issues and the very nature of the human experience. This may sound like a turnoff to many, but smarts and looks in one woman always does this to me.

I wanted the evening to last forever, so I could take my time getting to know Ashley and build up the expectation of being physically intimate with this gem. This wasn't so much sex as it was pure and sensual eroticism. Words just can't describe what my date with Ashley was like. So, rather than go into more detail and describe every act, I will simply say, if you want a real, down-to-earth, smart, sensual, naturally beautiful woman, then go see Ashley. I'm going to be seeing her again and again because I have a feeling she's the type of woman who seems sexier and sexier the more you get to know her.

My high-paying clients kept coming back for more, which pleased Anna to no end. And with the money I was raking in, I couldn't complain, either.

high-flying clients

The men whom Anna supplied with young women operated at a much higher level—often a global level. They wanted someone whom they could bring to dinner with friends, with whom they'd feel comfortable being photographed or escorting to social gatherings. A woman who was beautifully dressed and conversant in current events. Someone who would seem like a date, a girlfriend, with no one having a clue that a monetary transaction had taken place.

One of my first clients was a highly successful owner of the kind of nightclubs where celebrities and athletes were willing to pay $350 bottle-service fees for Stoli or $2,500 for Louis XIII de

Rémy Martin. His business had thrived in New York, and he was now expanding to other cities and thinking about venturing into the boutique hotel business.

My client—let's call him Steve—mingled with celebrities all the time, as it was his business, but they also seemed to be his pals. I chatted with them, and we all posed together for the tabloid photographers. Once, in a box at a Knicks game, I said I wanted a ball autographed by one of the players and I wanted it by halftime. I was just pretending to be a spoiled little princess—I didn't even have a clue who was playing for the Knicks at the time. But just as the third quarter began, in walked a team rep and handed me an autographed ball. Steve was sending me the message that I could have whatever I wanted. Next time I would be more ambitious!

After a night out in the city, Steve would often suggest to some of his friends and his friends' girlfriends—or "dates," like me—that we continue the party at his house in the Hamptons. We'd all head out to Steve's spacious estate, complete with pool, tennis court, and basketball court. No one used either of the courts that I saw, but every night when the boys were fast asleep, the girls would sit in the pool or Jacuzzi, drinking champagne.

One night, we all gathered in the living room, with its extra-wide custom couches done in neutral colors like "dune" and "seagrass." As the sun settled into the horizon, Steve headed to his Hawaiian bamboo bar and began making cocktails. He had started out as a bartender and was still proud of his mixology skills.

Someone started teasing Max—a guy with a Ferrari and a dozen other "important" sports cars—about how his cars were housed under better conditions than most of the people working for him. He was a member of an exclusive car club, where collectors kept their elite rides in an immaculate, guarded, and temperature- and humidity-controlled space. Each car had its own video camera pointed at it so the owner could look at it longingly online any time of the day or night. "Max just wants to be alone so he can drool over his Alfa Romeo Spider," said one coarse fellow with a Brooklyn accent. All the men laughed.

Steve brought a Balinese hammered-silver box over to the glass coffee table and gingerly opened it to reveal that it was filled nearly to the top with a white powder. "Me first!" said the Brooklyn guy as he took the razor blade and expertly portioned out three lines. He picked up one of several little glass tubes and snorted up the powder through it. "Go Knicks!" he cried, passing another tube to his date and shoveling out more lines. Everyone took their turn snorting up a line in each nostril, and then Steve turned to me and asked, "Ashley? Colombian marching powder?"

I did not believe in doing *any* kind of drug with clients, but they were more than welcome to do what they wanted. Unless it was hard-core, like crystal meth, or if it made them get out of control and put me in danger.

This wasn't really a request. I'd already learned that, for Steve, coke was foreplay. But I was ready for him.

"Absolutely," I said, smiling, and dangled a jeweled silver snorting tube I wore as a pendant. I snorted two lines into it, but it never went up my nose. I'd lined it with Vaseline that morning—a trick Kristin Davis had taught me early in the business because she knew I didn't do drugs. She didn't either, so she knew all the tricks to teach me. I was feeling grateful to her at that moment. Actually, each time I used that trick, I thought of her. Acting appropriately amorous, I sat back down next to Steve, lightly rubbing my breasts over his arm as I cuddled closer. We soon said good night to the group, and he took me by the hand to his bedroom. It was in another entire wing of his house.

He put on some music as I slipped into the shower to freshen up and put on some really special lingerie. An incredible guitar soloist came on. "Who is that?!" I called out. "Al Di Meola," he exulted. "That's 'Mediterranean Sundance.'"

"Wow," I said as I strutted into the room in a feathery black thong, black-lace push-up bra, and killer six-inch Christian Louboutin stilettos with patent-leather spikes. "He's the best."

"No, baby," said Steve as he ran his hand over my bottom. "You are."

The next morning, after a swim in Steve's pool, it was mimosas and omelets made to order by Steve's personal chef. Some weekends we'd linger, but this time Steve had a meeting in the city, and his driver pulled up in an Escalade to take us to East Hampton Airport in Wainscott for the chopper ride back to Manhattan.

"Some of us have to work for a living!" Steve yelled out the window to his buddies as they all guffawed.

Yes, some of us do. After a weekend of partying, I was $10,000 richer.

The next day I had my court-supervised visitation with my daughter. A woman whom I apparently paid to sit there and give me stern looks sat off to the side as Isabella and I drew with pastels. Isabella made a drawing of a rainbow with us holding hands beneath it, smiling, and little hearts all around us. Then, on a smaller piece of paper, she wrote in tiny letters *Take me home, Mama* and secretly passed it to me. It was all I could do not to burst into tears. Trying to keep my two lives separate was so difficult mentally. The character names I went by helped remarkably, but I didn't know how much longer I could keep it up.

Anna was extremely happy with me. I was "bringing it." She started a joint operation with a madam in London, and I was one of the girls she sent over. It was a simple matter of going overseas and staying in an apartment for a week at a time and being the "fresh new face." Being foreign was great. The British men are just like any others; they want and need good sex, and the all-American look was my selling point.

The escorts in London came in from all over the world. They all were doing what I was: meeting the most eligible men in Britain, or at least the men who were in town that week. Keeping their identity a secret is one of the biggest priorities in the United Kingdom, and men pay top dollar—or should I say pound—to ensure it stays that way. The entire purpose was to work. Making money was the goal, not making friends.

The same held true for London as it did for anywhere else. I'd accompany the client to dinner, the theater, or even overnight to Paris for a business dinner. Thank goodness at that point I had the wardrobe to pull it off.

In exchange for sending one of her American girls to London, Anna would get a European or British girl from the madam in the U.K. It was good business for them both, and kept clients on either side of the pond happy with lots of fresh new faces. That's what they loved and paid the most for.

•   •   •

A few of my clients were very eccentric. There was an Orthodox Jewish man who was always paranoid that there was someone in the East Seventy-Eighth Street apartment where I did the occasional incall for Anna. He'd check every single room, again and again. I would show up, sit down, and watch him run around and freak out, asking, "Are you sure there is no one here? How do you know, have you checked? Did you check the closets? Underneath the bed?" This would happen over and over. Once, he checked the place for the entire hour, never had sex, paid, and left. Best client ever to have.

Then there was the famous classical pianist who would call whenever he was in town to play Carnegie Hall. One time he asked the booker to send as many girls as possible, and we were all to bring our bikinis to wear in his hotel suite. At his request, we set up blankets on the floor and pretended to sunbathe. He started off swatting our bottoms with a towel, and then he would tickle us and chase us around the suite, still swatting us with the towel, and would watch us jump up and down on the bed with our tops off. Then he wanted us to chase him around and finally pull off the towel he was wearing, to reveal that he was aroused beneath. And then the game was over. I suppose everyone has their own fantasy.

Some clients needed therapy as much as they needed sex. They needed someone to talk to who was totally out of their world.

One such client was a young Middle Eastern prince. He was in his thirties. He had unlimited funds, but he was still depressed, because he was out of the power loop in his extended family. Older brothers and cousins were ahead of him in line for the throne. I learned a lot about Middle Eastern politics from him. Unfortunately for him, he developed a real nose-candy problem. He would stay at the Plaza Hotel, and they would hang the flag of his country out front. I wonder if New York coke dealers watched for it and made a beeline for the golden front doors. He did tremendous amounts of cocaine when we were together. The more he talked about his family, the more blow he snorted. He used to be able to go all night, and the last time I saw him he was so dissipated he couldn't even perform. Unlimited money doesn't always bring happiness.

When you're a high-end call girl, you can never let on that you have multiple clients.

No man wants to feel like he is one of many. They want to be the *only* one. The only way to do that is to make them feel special, and that is to offer the true GFE: the Girl Friend Experience. You French-kiss them, cuddle, go out on a date, hang out, talk, have passionate sex—whatever they want to do. You are their girlfriend for the night. Period. And you do anything to make them believe that. You have to *remember* how each and every man wants you to be. Often, their wives or girlfriends don't understand them, or appreciate them, and you do. You remember that they had this big deal coming up. You recall that they were going to Dubai on business. You notice the little things, like their Mercury-dime cuff links. You care. That's where the money is. Every single memory is a dollar sign.

The clients specified to Anna what sort of dress they desired. Some might want casual—jeans and heels with a sexy top; if I was going on a yacht, resort wear. My Europeans had higher expectations when going out to dinner. Same with the Wall Streeters. Out of necessity, I had to build an extensive wardrobe, and it became very costly.

Certain clients would give me carte blanche to buy whatever I wanted. Once the new Louis Vuitton ostrich boots came out, I told one of my dear clients how much I loved them. He replied, "Then get a pair." I just had to go to the Louis Vuitton store and charge him. He didn't blink at the $4,500 price tag. As long as I wore them on our next date.

I had three personal shoppers at Saks: one for clothing, one for shoes, and one for bags. And the ladies at the Chanel makeup counter know me well. The shoppers put together matching outfits for me. One of my clients would foot the bills.

My personal shoe shopper really knew what I liked. I'd buy $5,000 worth of shoes at a time. Sexiest shoes ever. She'd ship them to my house and bill my client, or I'd pay for them and he'd reimburse me in cash.

I'd always follow my shopping sprees with a spa treatment or a highlights appointment at Elizabeth Arden—the "Red Door" farther up Fifth Avenue. The aestheticians would see me coming and then surround me and dig through my shopping bags at the trove of goodies and squeal. Afterward I'd just call my client's chauffeur, and he'd pick me up in one of his Bentleys—he had four of them—to take me home. I needed it, because walking down Fifth Avenue in five-inch heels with all those bags was not happening.

Some view the materialism of call girls who have become infamous in recent years as amoral. But my clients required such things in order for me to keep them interested in me. If I did not meet their standards, I could easily be replaced by one of the hundreds of girls waiting in line to take my place, and I still had to make as much money as possible. Within a couple years, despite all the money I had made, I still had huge amounts of debt that seemed impossible to pay. I was losing my apartment and still fighting for custody of my daughter in court. There was a never-ending demand for money. Yet I was climbing the ladder so high in the business, and I realized there was a formula to making it to the very top.

Eventually, I had a client who set me up in an apartment. He is a major capitalist on a global scale, and sits on several corporate boards. He only had time to visit me two or three times a month, but the apartment's cost was lunch money to him. I refused to live there. It was merely a meeting place.

Once, we flew to Europe on his private Gulfstream to look over a castle. "What do you think?" he asked. "Should I buy it?"

Some of my clients said they'd fallen in love with me. They wanted me to stop seeing other clients and be their real (free) girlfriend. I didn't want anyone to fall in love with me. I wanted the money to keep coming in. There was one guy, William, whom I had begun to see in the Kristin days. He was in the middle of a divorce. He was in finance. You could see lines around his eyes, due to stress. He had lots and lots of money. We'd get together at the Four Seasons. Our first night together was a lot of fun. I ended up staying most of the night. I could tell he had a good time. He kept coming back. He'd find me wherever I was working—New York, Boston, Philadelphia, D.C. Once, in New York, he called and said, "I really want you to come to this concert tonight. I don't want sex. I just came to town to ask you to go to the concert with me." He felt I was in the wrong industry. This may sound harsh, but he is what we girls in the business call a Save-A-Ho guy. Like Richard Gere in *Pretty Woman*. They want to make "honest women" out of us. But I didn't want to be saved. I didn't need to be saved. I needed to save my little girl.

There was one client who tried to monopolize me. He was the man who set me up in an apartment. He also paid me a large sum of money at the beginning of every month. Yes, he was extremely generous. But I didn't feel that that entitled him to be my only client. He tried to own me. He felt he should be able to pick up the phone and that I should be ready in ten minutes. Twenty-four hours a day. He'd send his car and driver on a whim, and I was supposed to jump in and get over to him to have sex. There actually weren't many times when I felt like a prostitute. But one day he made me feel like one. He said, "I don't pay you to piss me off." He made me feel just horrible. I just hung up on him. That was the end of our "relationship." It was early in the month, but I kept that money. Screw him. Or not.

On the opposite end of the spectrum, I had a client who had inherited his own luxury company. I'll call him Jeffrey. He was married with children. He was a no-intercourse client. He viewed intercourse as cheating. But he wanted oral sex. Very much. His wife would never do it.

He always wanted to finish by ejaculating on my face. I found that somewhat degrading, but I acted like I loved it. He still would want me to spend the night, though, so he would get a room in the city for us. He commuted in, so I'm not sure what he told his family, but I loved falling asleep next to him. He liked holding me, and I liked it too. I think I was just feeling really lonely, and he was kind. He also liked to e-mail before and after sessions to either get him excited or give him something to keep going until the next time we would meet. He always dreamt that we were married and that we had a family, so I would type out little fantasies for him and he would reciprocate.

He was a generous guy. He paid my tuition to school. He sent the check directly to the school. He also gave me money for books and expenses. He liked that I was a student, doing something with my life. I was a little more open with him for some reason. He also wanted to make sure I had rest time. Whenever he saw that I was getting stressed out, he'd ask me where I wanted to go on vacation and how much it would cost for me and a friend to go. He would messenger over the cash to cover my entire vacation. He sent me to Jamaica and St. Lucia many times. I've met his family. They think I'm wonderful. They don't know who I am to him.

One client had a friend, a very famous mogul, who was very, very rich. But he was lonely. Still active in business, but elderly. An ideal combination for an enterprising girl. Out of chivalry, my client introduced another call girl he was seeing to his friend. He actually gave the girl tips and primed her before the introduction. The call girl and the mogul hit it off and got married, and now she's set for life.

My client offered to do the same thing for me. I knew that

what he was offering would solve all of my problems financially for life. But even though I mentally "flip the switch" to do this job as "Ashley," when Rebecca is back, I believe in true love and that one day, I will get married, and it will be because I am in love with a man who is in love with me. I still believe that, even after all that I have done and seen. There are actually several famous socialites often pictured in *Town & Country* and the society pages of the *New York Times* who started out working for madams in Paris, London, and New York. I didn't want to be a hooker for life either.

I had another client who was so dependent on me that he flew me to Tokyo for just one session. I met Edward all over the world, in cities where he would fly on business. He was a major financier and probably bore partial responsibility for the crash of 2008. He paid me big money, more and more over time. But I discovered later that he was a very sick man.

He always preferred it if I came up with a sexual scenario. He liked to be surprised. He gave me an unlimited budget for outfits—leather, rubber, and the like. Toys. I had a closet full of gear just for him.

Once, Edward was on his way to Japan from London for a meeting and had his assistant book me at the Conrad in Tokyo for two nights. He said he'd be very busy during the day and that I could do whatever I wanted.

The only expectation was that I'd be available for a certain period of time in the evening for an hour or two, maximum. We set up an approved time.

I had a suite. The view of Tokyo was spectacular. The

bathroom floor was heated. I waited there, and he finally called in the wee hours. I said, "Too bad, you missed your window." I was in charge in this particular relationship, and that's what he paid for. He had to obey. Don't be surprised. I've found that guys who have a lot of power they feel they don't deserve often want to be dominated. Sometimes he'd get scared about what he asked for. He was a very tormented guy. He apologized profusely and said he'd see me the next night.

I woke up early in the morning and took one of those silly bus tours. I hooked up with a group from Wisconsin. But I jumped off at Takeshita-dori, the home of teenage Harajuku fashion, to pick up some things for Isabella. Edward always said that anytime I went somewhere as his guest I could go shopping and get anything I wanted and just give him the receipts. So I headed to Omotesando, Tokyo's Fifth Avenue, and bought myself a peacock-colored pearl necklace scattered with diamonds. Why not?

I went back to the hotel, and he did come over that evening. I had packed certain sex toys that he had asked me to purchase. I followed his instructions for our Tokyo encounter. One of the first things I did was tie his wrists to the headboard. Then I put tiny clothespins around the rim of his penis. The more aroused he got, the more I punished him. That's what he liked. That's what he paid me $25,000 for.

But then, after two years of sessions like this, during which I never balked at his stranger and stranger requests, he asked me something that turned my stomach. "Ashley," he said, "would you be able to get me a young boy?"

"*What?*" I cried. "Absolutely not! You disgust me!" I grabbed my things to leave. "And you can forget about seeing me ever again!"

"Ashley, wait!" he said, and started to cry like a baby.

"Get the hell away from me and get yourself some help," I said as I ran out, checked out, and headed to the airport. It took me the whole flight back to recover. I worried: Would Anna acquiesce to his request?

where are you taking me?

A little over a year went by and I still had not won custody of Isabella. The case dragged on. I could tell during court appearances that Mike was tiring of the battle—or, more likely, the expense of the battle. We were both paying thousands of dollars a month in legal bills.

Just as I began to get more unsupervised time with Isabella in my custody fight, just as I was carving out an identity as a PTA leader, my world came crashing down. The investigators for then Manhattan district attorney Robert Morgenthau found me as soon as Kristin was busted. They didn't arrest me, but I was called in for questioning to One Hogan Place, the DA's headquarters at the state criminal courthouse. Nobody told me to bring a lawyer. I took the subway downtown and had plenty of time on the journey to contemplate my imminent loss of freedom and, worse, my daughter. I was a nervous wreck when I arrived. Would I be arrested now? Prostitution is a class B misdemeanor in New York State: I could get three months in jail! My custody battle for Isabella would be lost.

I went through the metal detectors and up to a dreary floor lined with green and gray metal filing cabinets right out of a forties noir film. It looked as if they hadn't bought a new desk in decades. I was led into a room with a plain gray metal table, a few raggedy chairs, and a horrific fluorescent light overhead.

Two men came in, and one sat at the table in front of me. "Miss Kade," said one. "I am Assistant District Attorney Artie McConnell, and this is . . ." My mind went on overbuzz at the words "assistant district attorney" and I didn't even catch the other man's name. He looked like he'd graduated law school the week before and appeared to be less important, as he sat on the side of the room and not at the table where Mr. McConnell and I were sitting facing one another.

"Ms. Kade, we have asked you to come in today because we would like to discuss a few things with you regarding your relationship with Kristin Davis. As you are probably aware, she was arrested recently, and we are prosecuting her on several charges and talking to people who knew her. Your name has come up, but we anticipate this to be a relatively short interview. I have a document here for you to sign. It is a debriefing agreement, and it merely states that you are free to leave at any time and that statements you make during this interview could be used in a future prosecution. However, any statement you make today cannot be used to prosecute you in the future." I signed the document, but to be honest, I didn't have a clue what he had just said or what that document was supposed to mean to me. I just heard my sister's voice saying *Tell the truth,* and that was what I was going to do.

Mr. McConnell and his assistant started interrogating me.

Had I worked as an escort for Kristin Davis?

"Yes." They obviously knew I had or I wouldn't be there.

"Have you worked for anyone else, and if so, who?" McConnell asked.

"Ummm, a company called Classic Affairs," I answered hesitantly.

"God, these names are so clichéd. Who runs it?"

I stalled. "A woman . . . named Anna." I did not want to answer that question. I thought this was going to be purely about Kristin! Now I would be implicating myself with another madam? He put his pen down, and he and the other man looked at each other and nodded.

"Will you excuse us for a minute?" McConnell said, and they both walked out of the room and shut the door. That was it? They had only asked me a couple of questions, and the tone in the room had completely changed. After a few minutes they came back in. "We're going to have to transfer you to another location, Ms. Kade," said McConnell.

"You can't be here anymore," he said sternly as he shut the door behind him so no one could see inside the room.

"Why?" I asked.

"We'll have to explain that to you later," he said. "We're going to have some people escort you out of the building to an unmarked car. We will make sure you will be covered so no one can see you leaving the building. We're taking you to a safer location."

"*What? Why?*" I sputtered.

"They'll explain it when you get there. Come on," he said, taking my arm.

"No!" I said, pulling back. "I'm not going anywhere until I know what's going on and someone in my family knows where I'm going."

I called my sister and gave her a quick rundown of where I was and that I was going to another location. I told her I had a signed document giving me rights that I would mail to her as we were leaving the building. I didn't trust these guys, and I felt uncomfortable having paperwork like that in my apartment. She instructed me again to tell the truth.

After a few minutes, three big guys with gold detectives' badges on thin metal chains hanging around their necks came in and said my time was up on the phone.

"OK, Bridget, I have to go," I said. "You should hear from me tonight. If you don't, you know something went wrong." I was thinking, *This is ridiculous. What is going on? Why are they being so dramatic?* I felt as if I were being pulled into a movie.

"You have to come with us now," said the biggest of the cops. They slipped a lanyard with an orange ID card on it around my neck. Then they threw my coat over my head and led me past the old green metal filing cabinets down a dingy hallway to an elevator bank, then down and out the side door of the courthouse. They had me surrounded, my coat still over my head. They put me in the back of a car, one cop on either side, and we sped off. I was terrified.

In the unmarked car, they took my coat off my head. I wasn't handcuffed. I asked right then and there, "Am I being arrested?" They assured me that I was not—in fact, far from it. They said that I wasn't safe in that building. They said it was very possible that I had important information they had been looking for in an investigation, and that there were concerns that there might be a leak or mole in their own office. They wanted to get me out before anyone knew I was there. I never saw ADA McConnell again.

It's very possible that someone in the district attorney's office had been warning Anna as they cracked down on other madams and pimps. Maybe someone there was a client. I don't know what the explanation was, but somehow Anna had gone unscathed.

I was more confused than ever. What the hell did I know that was so damn important that they had to cover my head with my coat, throw me in the back of a car, and speed off from the Manhattan district attorney's office to some secret location? *This has to be a joke,* I thought. The only problem was, I didn't know any of these people, so why would they want to play a joke on me? The driver cruised past the Metropolitan Correctional Center and then we were navigating the streets of Chinatown, past barkers on Canal Street who were openly bringing tourists into rooms behind false walls in their shops to buy counterfeit watches and purses as the cops cruised by. The vegetable stands disappeared, and soon we passed luxury leather goods boutiques and galleries as we drove farther down the cobblestone streets of SoHo. Were we headed to another precinct? Suddenly, in the middle of SoHo, we stopped in front of an old converted warehouse, got out, and took the renovated elevator upstairs into a gigantic, light-filled loft. No old metal filing cabinets there. I learned later that it had been seized from a drug dealer and was now a secret special investigations headquarters.

"Where am I?" I demanded after they took me into a cramped office.

"You are in the Official Corruption Unit of the Manhattan District Attorney's Office," said one investigator. "You mentioned a person who we have been investigating for quite some time: Anna. Can you tell us anything about her?"

I knew I had valuable information. I was one of the few girls Anna had allowed to get close to her. But I didn't want to talk about her, and I certainly wasn't about to name clients. Not only had these men kept me afloat, but I was terrified that Anna would find out and come after me. As scared as I was of being arrested, tried, and jailed, I still was not prepared to give them clients' names.

The investigators asked me questions about the business. How was I paid? Did I work over state lines? Did I work internationally? Was drug dealing involved?

"Why should I tell you anything?" I demanded. "She's your best friend if you're nice to her, but if you cross her, she's a killer. Just ask Jason Itzler."

Itzler was the self-styled "King of All Pimps," who once had Ashley Alexandra Dupré, the girl who brought down Eliot Spitzer, working at his agency, New York Confidential. Itzler claimed that Gristina had sent three thugs, one of them armed, to threaten him and scare girls out of working for him instead of her. Itzler would later tell a New York tabloid, "She's the most vindictive bitch in the escorting game. Dangerous, dangerous, dangerous."

"Well, Ms. Kade, we already have evidence that you worked

as a prostitute through your connection with Kristin Davis. If we prosecute you and you are convicted, you could get a jail sentence."

I'd never get Isabella back if that happened. So I made my decision—one that would determine the next four years of my life.

my life as a confidential
informant begins

The Manhattan district attorney's investigators already knew that Anna regularly boasted that she had law enforcement connections. Sultry Irma Nici, who claimed to have had sex with David Beckham and who'd worked for Anna for six months, had already told prosecutors as much.

That's part of what kept Anna in business so long, some surmised, and that's why the Official Corruption Unit, rather than the Sex Crimes Unit—the one once headed by the famous prosecutor turned mystery writer Linda Fairstein—was in charge of the investigation.

The investigators asked me more questions that day, and the

next. They showed me a lot of surveillance photos to see if I could ID anyone. This went on for days, then weeks. They would drive me home at the end of the day, then pick me up first thing the next morning to be interrogated again.

I was missing so much school that they had to write me an excuse, like in high school: "Miss Kade was witness to a serious crime in the recent past," they wrote. "She [has had to] report to our office. . . . These duties consumed a great deal of Ms. Kade's time."

I was missing school by day, but by night I was still working for Anna. I was still working as an escort, and the prosecutors knew it. I would eventually learn why they had allowed me to keep breaking the law.

"What is Anna's last name?" the ADA grilled me.

"Who knows what her real name is?" I answered. "She's gone by Anna Tennant, Anna Gristina, Anna Scotland. She was born in Scotland; I doubt that name's real."

It was clear to me that the investigators had very little information on Anna, and they pumped me for as much as they could. I told them what I knew about the business, the key players, but I did not give up clients' names. They pressured me with photo lineups, and it was when I saw the photo of Edward—my pedophile client—that I had a breakdown in their office. Just seeing his face caught me off guard, and I cried hysterically. Feeling somewhat relieved, I revealed the truth about him.

"Ms. Kade, we want you to do something for us," one of the prosecutors told me after weeks of questioning.

"What more do you want?" I practically cried in exasperation.

"We want you to start recording your conversations with

Anna Gristina," he said. "We want you to gather some evidence for us."

Wait, I thought. *Isn't that the job of an undercover cop? Like on TV, when a beautiful young female cop only pretends to go work for an escort service? How the hell would I pull that off?* I was terrified. They made it seem as if I had a choice. But I didn't.

I couldn't fathom how a wiretap would work. First of all, there was the matter of Anna's preference for texts over phone calls. She changed her phone numbers constantly, and if she ever did call you, it would usually be brief and to the point. But the investigators had a lot of specific questions they wanted me to ask her that would lead to her arrest and conviction. It was true that Anna had started to open up to me. She would call me from her farm upstate to book a high-level client, and we'd end up having long, friendly conversations. But how was I going to suddenly ask her *Law & Order*–type questions in the middle of a gal-pal chat? Not to mention that, while alone at my house, I would have to manage outdated tape recorders, the only equipment the technical department had after years of city budgetary cutbacks.

The prosecutors wanted me to record Anna talking all about her clients, her girls, how she ran the business, the law enforcement connections she boasted about, and what she had done about the child predator's request.

I was scared. Anna is your best friend when you're on her good side, but she will slit your throat if you cross her.

What's more, Anna had become increasingly cautious, even paranoid, ever since Andreia Schwartz had been deported. Andreia, a pretty Brazilian escort turned madam who had worked at the Emperor's Club V.I.P. agency with Eliot Spitzer's call girl Ashley Dupré, had been deported in March 2008 after serving eighteen months in prison. Spitzer's use of escorts, uncovered by the FBI, had led to the sweep by the Manhattan DA that brought down Kristin. Andreia would end up serving time in a predominantly male sex offenders' unit on Rikers Island and forfeit half a million dollars after pleading guilty to promoting prostitution, a class D felony, in October 2008. (Cecil Suwal owned Emperor's Club V.I.P. with her boyfriend, Mark Brener, forty years her senior. It was the Emperor's Club V.I.P. listing of my client Eliot Spitzer as their Client No. 9 that led to the New York governor's resignation.) Anna believed that Andreia had informed on her, and now she was keeping a low profile by isolating herself on her upstate farm. It would be too suspicious for me to visit her there.

"We'll have to try wiretapping a phone call," said Morgenthau's assistant district attorney on the case (and the first of several handlers I would work with).

They set up a wiretap on my phone, the one on which Anna always called to do business or just to chat. I would have to use every skill set I had to elicit the kind of information the ADA wanted in the middle of a girlfriend-to-girlfriend call.

The other form of communication that Anna was using was Skype. She found it useful because it couldn't be traced and was completely safe—or so she thought. It would be extra tricky for me because Skype calls are video chats, so she could see everything I was doing.

One of the first conversations I had with Anna was in early April of 2008. It was the call I was waiting for: Kristin had just been arrested, and Anna wanted to check in and make sure I was OK. I was in my bedroom doing homework in my yoga clothes when the phone rang and I saw her personal number pop up. I froze, but then sprang into action. I'd attached the wires to each connector of my cell phone and left them that way when I was at home so I would never miss a word. My heart pounding, I pushed RECORD on the equipment, put the earpiece in my ear, and laid out the ADA's talking points in front of me. My life as a confidential informant had begun.

recording the "soccer mom madam"

was so nervous, I could barely say "Hello."

Anna was nervous, too, but not about talking to me. She was in freak-out mode, as all the high-level madams and pimps in town were getting busted, one by one. She was furious at the thought that someone might have turned on her. The conversation I recorded went like this:

A: I have good news. I'm not on any "stop-and-hold" list. I'm not on any federal list or any state list. I had my friend at Customs run my name on the computer. I had them run my green card number, my passport number, and everything. That means I can come and go. But still, do you ever get the harrowing feeling something's not right?

I couldn't believe she said that while I was wiretapping her. If I wasn't so nervous, I might have burst out laughing.

R: Right now, I get that all the time.

A: Seriously! I woke up in the middle of the night with my heart pounding. And I don't know why. I woke my husband up. I just get this feeling that I need to leave town and be gone for a little while. I said, "Something's going down." I said, "I can't tell you how I know that."

That little cunt Andreia Schwartz is the reason Kristin and all these places got busted. Kristin's name was on the list. My name, as Anna Scotland, was on the list. She didn't have my real name.

R: The Kristin I know?

A: Yes. The Brazilian worked for Kristin also. Yes, she did. So her and I got into a squabble. I was at the top of her You're-fucked list.

Now, a good friend of mine who is at the precinct in New Jersey, the FBI holding center, where they do interrogation and federal stuff—where Schwartz was being held the last week of her stay in the U.S. . . . that friend of mine, let's just say his brother has been on the force for thirty years and he's one of the head guys in the FBI down in Jersey. Get my drift? He just registered "Anna Scotland," and I had told my friend that I was in a fight with this girl, so he knew my name. He didn't know my last name. He hired a PI called Vincent Parco, who's a motherfucker. He tracked me down through an old medical insurance card I used to have years ago to a PO box. I don't have one piece of mail or one bill come to my location of residence. I've always looked over my shoulder because I always knew. You know what I mean?

You're going to ask me, well, how did he get my name? Well, I'm going to tell you how he got my real name: that motherfucker attorney, Brian O'Malley,* who represents all madams and hookers in New York. He was one of my clients in a free fucking service, and then this whole thing happened and he tried to shake me down. I said, "What were you seeing? A girl from me every week. Or every two weeks. You were there for two hours. It cost me $800. Now you want to milk me? You want $4,000 to make this thing go away? No, no, no." I think I was right, don't you?

R: Absolutely!

A: So, guess what? That motherfucker turned in my name and telephone number. And they tracked it to my billing address. That's how they got my PO box. Then they had my real name. They were able to track my Social Security number through my medical insurance.

R: You're a citizen?

A: Yeah, I'm legal here. I'm American and British, honey. I've got two passports. I've always had that. I'm 100 percent legal. I pay taxes. I do the whole thing.

Anyway, the reason I knew it was Brian O'Malley is because I found out through a friend of mine who works at the *New York Post* that Brian O'Malley was representing this girl called Julia, and Julia was part of the case with Andreia

---

* Not his real name.

Schwartz. I put one and one together and got two. Parco has the spelling of my name wrong, but he knows where my PO box is. That's the only information Brian had. And the way that Brian has continued to spell my name wrong was the way Parco spelled it when he sent a [false] letter. You know what I mean? You know when you just get a feeling?

I managed to blurt out "Uh-huh!" Anna's instincts were better than good—she didn't know how good.

What became interesting to me later was that Anna hired Vincent Parco—the private eye she had called a "motherfucker" in this phone call—to help her during her own trial in 2012. Maybe she thought Parco had just been doing his job—and a good one at that. She was more furious with her lawyer, an apparent sex-business litigator who felt he could improve his expertise with in-depth research in the field. But in the rest of the call, she revealed the tough side of herself that hardly jibes with the warm-and-fuzzy soccer mom image she projected during her trial:

A: This Brian O'Malley is going to get so fucked. I've got credit cards, the receipts that link him to Las Vegas. I've got girls who I know for a fact would come forward. At least three girls from Vegas who would say, "That motherfucker, this is what he did." I just don't want to make enemies. But I know that it's because of [him]. He represents anything hooker related: massage parlors, escorts, hookers on the street, anything to do with girls in the industry. He was with Julia's case, and that was tied to Andreia Schwartz. And all of a sudden Vincent Parco has my address. Isn't that just convenient?

Anna was implying here that her lawyer had given prosecutors her name in exchange for leniency for his client, Julia, after Anna balked at his bill after years of providing him with hooker services for free.

I couldn't believe she was chatting on about all this as the tape rolled. I felt a twinge of guilt, but I struggled to keep my focus.

A: That's OK. You know what I did? I sicced the media on him. [Laughs.] A reporter showed up at his office and said, "I hear that you are actually a client and you're a 'friend with benefits' with many of the madams." He denied it.

But I will get him for this. Revenge is a dish best served cold. This Brazilian girl has made a big hassle in my life. But I understand she really thought I had something to do with [her arrest]. I probably would have done the same thing if I were her. I feel bad for her, to be honest. I don't even dislike her. I hope she moves on with her life and learns from this.

But Brian O'Malley? He was my attorney. I paid him great money. He saw girls through me at no cost, out of my pocket. Then the motherfucker handed my name over to a private investigator on another case he was working on? Is that ethical?

R: How could he do that?

A: Because he was making money from the other case.

R: That was really dumb on his part.

A: It was never enough for Brian. I paid for his air ticket. He got a VIP suite in the Harrah's hotel [in Las Vegas], all on my credit card. He's forgetting that. It will come back. You just have to trust me. Things always come back. I don't even really care. I just want to have a peaceful life. I'm out of it now.

Brian O'Malley knew [my name and address]. He met my husband 'cause he did some work for my husband. Incorporation papers and stuff. 'Cause my husband had his own business. He went to lunch with my husband. My husband made the mistake of saying, "My brother is high up in law enforcement." He is . . . He's one of the head investigators. Get my drift? [Brian] told that to Parco; Parco told it to the FBI months ago when that cunt [Andreia Schwartz] was giving out names. My name came up.

The FBI agent told my guy, "You need to tell your Scottish friend she needs to leave town for quite a while." Get my drift? The next day my brother-in-law called my husband from a pay phone. He said, "I was watching the news the other night and a lot of things are going on in the industry. Your wife's out of town, right?" Get my drift? He [Anna's husband, Kelvin Gorr] goes, "Yeah, the strangest thing, there's been a Crown Victoria car that's been sitting at the end of my road for the last day and a half. It's got New Jersey plates. The plates have a funny bogus name that's federal. That's how they do it, right?"

My husband's other brother has been in the sheriff's department for, like, fourteen years. He's the captain. He doesn't even know what I do for a living. Nothing. My two brothers-in-law were speaking. One says, "I have this Crown Victoria." He says, "That's funny, I have one too." That's when we ran the plates [of the car in her driveway] and discovered they were federal, [headquartered] out of New Jersey. It was registered to the bogus company that the feds register cars to. My brother-in-law—the one that knows a little bit about what I do—was perplexed. He says to my husband, "You know, it's a good time to migrate. I hear the birds are flying, because there's going to be singing soon. Spring is coming." You get my drift? You get the conversation, right? The next thing you know, my husband came home with a note. He didn't even talk. He said, "Time to go. *Now.*" I had had that feeling the night before. My husband had said it was crazy. Now I had fifteen minutes to pack my bags, grab my dog, and get the fuck out of the house. I didn't even have contact lenses with me. I had four pairs of underwear that my dog shredded. Every time I jump in the shower—I do it every time—don't you leave your underwear on the bathroom floor and pick them up when you come out? Well, my dog shreds them. You can use them as dental floss.

So I get up [to Montreal]. My husband, I call him a couple of days later. He says, "How are you enjoying where you are?" I said, "Uh, I'm not." He says, "Well, you'd better start to like it."

The good news is that if anyone tried to abduct my son at the school bus, I don't have to worry because he has an eye watching him all the time. He's being watched all the time. He was telling me there were people at the bottom of my driveway, across the street. Then one day my house got broken into. Then a maroon van just appeared with the New Jersey plate. So I think that little cunt talked about me; I think Vincent Parco gave up my name to the feds; the feds ran down the list to look and couldn't find anything and then moved on. Because there is nothing to find, Rebecca. They pulled my banking records in the U.S. I have nothing. They are so squeaky clean. Everybody has something; mine are so clean, they're almost too clean.

Bingo. I needed her to talk about her finances, and she'd led the conversation there herself. I tried to elicit more:

R: Aren't you worried about that part?

A: Look, I don't have a $2 million home and claim to make $30,000 a year. I didn't do that whole thing. Everything I ever buy or do has been in cash. I don't buy large purchases. I buy things in different names. I don't own anything in my own name. I don't own any cars.

R: Not even your new one?

A: No, that's in my other partner's corporation name. It's a corporate car. I get to use the corporate car but I don't own it. That's owned by the land development company my partner owns. He has no idea. . . .

For example, we have an American Express card and you claim you make $50,000 a year. But if you're doing $50,000 a year in charges, using your credit card, going on vacations, they'll think you're full of shit.

R: Yeah, because where are you getting that?

A: But we've never done that. I pay my kids' stuff in cash, like clothes and games. Everything has always been in cash. But all our bills have been paid from our checking account. I never had a flamboyant lifestyle. I never lived big like these other people. I never wanted to be.

Anyway, cutting a long story short, the good news is, they've looked into me and they've found nothing of interest and the lead has gone cold. They're putting it down to a disgruntled girl with a grudge.

R: That's good.

A: Yeah, but I'm still not coming back for a while. I'm still not comfortable. Would you be?

R: I get it. [Boy, did I.] No, I totally understand. It must be hard to be away from your family. At least you have your dogs, though.

I waited, but no, she would never talk about missing her family. Me, I wouldn't be able to stand it. How could she stay away like that? Maybe it hurt so much she couldn't express it.

A: The other thing, the option is that, if I came back, and there's something I could get tied to, there'd be no choice when I was going to come back.

R: Yeah, I hear you. But since I e-mailed you this morning, I looked at this whole Kristin thing. It doesn't even seem like it's a big deal anymore.

A: I was thinking that. Well, that's how I'm feeling. I'm sitting here thinking, OK, this bitch . . .

R: Two million dollars. They make it out like it's a huge thing. Then all of a sudden, a week later, it's no big deal? Where's the scary part of all this? I don't know . . .

A: The bottom line is they're on a witch hunt for Spitzer. Andreia Schwartz said, "Yes, I fucked Spitzer." Andreia Schwartz turned in some names. My name was on that list. I had a fight with her. They started following leads on the list she gave them; they staked out my place, realized there was nothing going on, because there's not. My kids go to school; my husband goes to work every day. I'm not even there. Get my drift? Even if they put my phones and everything at my home under surveillance, we never use them for anything. I've never once made a business call from my home phone number. I never would. I always had those 514 [the Montreal area code] numbers and disposable cells. You may laugh at those 514 numbers, but they're off the jurisdiction of U.S. subpoenas for surveillance. Did you know that?

R: No. Because they're out of the country?

A: Yeah.

R: Oh, that's a good idea.

A: That's why I had an office up in Canada. All my bills, all my phones, everything is billed out of here. And in case it comes to light, it's legal in Canada.

R: Oh, it is?

A: Yeah.

R: We should all move to Canada.

A: Yeah, but it's really cheap up here. It's, like, $300 an hour.

R: Oh, that sucks!

A: Anywhere you go, when something's legal, it becomes cheap. That's why we get so much in [New York].

Anyway, because this Brazilian girl had a thing for me, she gave my name up. Obviously, they've done their surveillance; they've realized after pulling all my records—and let me tell you, they pulled my bank records, they pulled everything— they feel there's nothing that shouldn't be there. There's no big money flying through my account, flamboyant trips, first-class trips, nothing like that.

R: My bank account record . . . Is that linked to some private account or is that your . . . I mean . . . I don't even look at that, so I don't really know.

Anna had made a couple of wire transfers into my bank account using the name Anna Tennant, and I was starting to worry, but I also thought I might be able to nail one of her accounts down. It had been for a payment for a trip to Tokyo. This would end up being a lead for the DA.

A: Can I be honest? You'll be happy to hear that it's located out-side of the country.

R: Oh, OK.

A: You want to hear a funny thing? It's not even my name. No, it's somebody else. But it's a good friend. It's cool. They're really good. It's the link to me, you know what I mean?

R: No, as I said, I've always said, the less I know the better.

A: You know what, Rebecca, you know what it is? I keep think-ing the FBI are looking for me because they're at the bottom of my driveway. I was scared. You seem to think every time the phone rings, or you hear the doorbell ring, maybe they're downstairs for you. Maybe our fears are taking the better of us. Maybe none of this is really going on and we're all just paranoid.

R: Yeah, I agree.

A: [Kristin] would not give your name up. I feel it in my heart. She would not do that to you.

R: I'm telling you, anybody else who got my name, if she gave a list of names, my name would be one of many. But if that [*New York Post* court reporter] Laura Italiano [finds out] . . .

A: I don't like her, either. She parties with Vincent Parco.

R: She does?

A: Yes, she does. Our lives are very [intertwined]. Our lives are not that far apart. I don't know if you're noticing that.

R: I'm starting to get that idea.

A: I know her editor in chief. Very, very well. But there's a price that comes with that. Do you understand?

R: Well, here's the question, OK? I have enough cash to get me through April at this point. If I have to come up with some-thing very fast, this is something I have to ask my sister for.

Do you have any idea what I'm going to have to come up
with?

A: [You mean] for an attorney?

R: No, you're saying there's a price to be paid.

A: Oh, not that type of price! That's illegal! No, no, no. It means,
if you know something about the case, or down the road, if
you hear anything illegal going on, you're going to have to
drop a little information.

R: Oh, OK. No problem.

A: It's called being a source. A newspaper source. You get my
drift, right?

R: But I don't know anything.

A: You think you don't. But you know frickin' Kristin; you know her
better than anybody.

R: I know.

A: I think it would be wrong at this point. Unless she gave up
your name. I think it would be wrong. I wouldn't do it. Well,
put it this way: if they came and knocked at my door, I swear
to you on my children's' lives, I will not let anybody take the
fall for my mistakes. I'd say, "I didn't keep names, I didn't
keep records." It really is the truth, Becca. If they were to look,
I couldn't even tell you the names of the girls I worked with.
Because I really didn't want to know. The only one I knew was
that bitch Andreia Schwartz, because she's been a nightmare
of mine for two years.

I knew this was coming. That's why I moved everything to
Canada. I changed my phone lines two years ago. As soon as
she got busted, I said, fuck that, she's going to be wanting to
give out names. I know my name will be at the top of her head
because we got into a fight. Lesson learned. I'll never fight with

people again. "OK, fine, you're angry. Sorry you feel that way. Good-bye." Never again.

I just don't think Kristin would give up your name. I just don't think she would. I think she'll give up this girl [Jessica] Cutler [the sex worker and blogger called "Washingtonienne," a friend of madam Kristin Davis], the one that's running her mouth . . .

R: But Jessica's already outed herself.

A: No, she's denying it. She says she was just a social acquaintance.

R: She's a publicity whore.

A: Nobody wants this kind of publicity. It's one thing if she bangs the governor and can write a tell-all book and make a million. But she didn't. She's nobody. This Jessica Cutler is a gossip that made enemies in Washington. I have no idea who she is. I didn't even know about her. I never heard about her before.

R: You never read her book?

A: No.

R: She wrote a book about the whole thing.

A: Lovely. Listen, I know you're going to be strapped about money. If I generate some old friends, like —— and a couple of other people, are you nervous, or do you want to sneak out and see some people? Off the record.

R: That's what I'm saying. You know how I feel about new clients.

A: Well, who was the last [one]?

R: Uh, that guy —— .

A: He was a regular from years ago. He's an artist.

R: Yeah.

A: If you're uncomfortable seeing anyone, I don't even want to bother. But you've said you're going to be really stressed about money after this month, correct?

R: I don't know what I'm going to do.

A: What about the guy —— downtown? I can call him. I can let —— know you're working. People you might want me to reach out to, I can reach out to them.

R: I know I kind of blasted the whole [expletive] thing. He probably doesn't want to see me after not wanting to see him.

A: I'm having trouble with him anyway. He's not making the money he used to.

R: Oh, really?

A: He makes money. But he would spend $10,000 a night. Now he won't even spend more than a couple of thousand. I think everybody's been hard hit with this recession.

But, no, listen, I think it's a time for caution. It's a time to be really, really careful and to stay away from the mainstream of the people. I only reach out to people I really trust.

R: I don't know. That's the thing.

A: I will never advertise as an agency again. Those days are gone.

R: Anybody who does that isn't very smart.

A: Did you see the big agencies? Oh my God, they have ads that are still up.

R: You think they're doing that because they think they can? Because they think everybody is so busy with Kristin?

A: The [prosecutors] are going to go through the list. They're even hitting body rubs. They're hitting everything. Kristin made such big waves because she was so flamboyant. That's what makes her an interesting media story. From what I've heard, she's not exactly a lady.

R: Really, now . . . Is anyone still around? Aren't they kind of stupid at this point?

A: Off the record, I knew this was all coming down. Not Kristin. But I left before any of this happened. I knew shit was coming. And there's more to come. There was a big place that got hit on Friday night and none of us know who it is. They didn't put it in the papers yet.

They made a boo-boo with Kristin. Her booker disappeared. They were supposed to get her at the same time they got Kristin. But something went wrong. It took them five days to find her. Did you know that?

R: Yeah, well, Grace was hiding at her apartment and went up to her mom's. That's what I read in the papers.

A: Don't read the papers. Even when you give them information, it's never what you told them!

R: I even read in the paper that Grace had been out for a long time.

A: I thought I read that. I don't know the girl.

R: I heard from people who still work for Kristin that is not true, that she was still there.

A: I know they're looking for a girl called Amanda. I don't know who she is.

R: I know who Amanda is. I met Amanda in the summer of 2006. When Kristin was expanding Philadelphia, she needed someone to run Philadelphia when she wasn't there. So she found this girl Amanda. Kristin and I went down for the weekend to kind of hang out and have drinks.

A: I wouldn't want to be Amanda. There's a manhunt for her.

R: She's a highlighted blonde. Shoulder-length hair. Probably about five-six. Working girl. Cute but not drop-dead gorgeous.

The very last call that I did for Kristin, she actually was on the call. So she kind of migrated from running Philadelphia to doing some work in New York. I don't know if she went back to that.

A: She was supposed to be running a lot of the operation.

R: There's Beth and there's Lucy. Where did Lucy go? Why is Lucy's name not out there? I haven't figured that one out.

A: It is. I saw it in the newspaper a couple of days ago. It was in the *Post*. They didn't say the name Lucy; they just had the name of her agency. Off the record, because the media doesn't know this, she changed the name of her agency.

R: I think Lucy is the scary one.

A: Why?

R: Because she knew too much information. I don't think she was just a booker. I think she was, like, Kristin's partner. . . . There's no way she had the kind of money to start that business.

A: Jason Itzler says he booked her. I can't even see him hiring her. She's . . . not to get too personal, but she's really creepy. I thought it was a guy they were showing pictures of. I really thought it was a guy.

R: Everybody is saying that.

A: She's really a woman, right?

R: Oh, yeah.

A: The only reason I ask that is cause she really looks like a man.

R: She goes for a lot of types of service, and I mean a lot of plastic surgery. I've seen her boobs, because she's changed in front of me, but I've never seen her crotch. Maybe I'm wrong, but I find it hard to believe that she's not a woman.

A: I'll keep in touch with my source at the paper. And I'll ask them to keep an eye on Laura [Italiano]. My friend at the *Post* owes me a lot of favors. I think they would kick something out if I said it was a personal favor. I've known her for fourteen years. My daughter is an intern down at the newspaper this summer. Doing it for summer credit. She's seventeen; she's going to be eighteen. She's either going to be there or at the other paper, the *New York Observer.* I'm not sure. Whatever would be best for her résumé. But she doesn't get paid to work there. She works there just for the credit. They let her go out in the field with the reporters. She can be in the office for four or five weeks. Every summer they invite four or five kids. Believe it or not, my daughter wants to do media, journalism.

Since I had a lot of connections, I was able, before any of this came up, to [arrange it]. They owed me a couple of big favors. I'm not the type of person who would turn over information that would hurt people. I wouldn't do that. But if they asked me "What do you know about this agency?" I'd say, well, not so great as they used to be. I try to be, how would you say, diplomatic. Because I know what it's like to be [in] the industry and be on both sides of the fence. I don't know Kristin. There's nothing I can ever say about her. But if they were to call me and ask me about a couple of other motherfuckers, like Jason Itzler, you're not kidding I gave out that information, and I fucking let him know I gave it too. Because I didn't care. He was a motherfucker. You know that Jason Itzler character, right?

R: Oh, yeah. Everybody does.

A: He's scary. He's claiming that Kristin worked for him as the rock-star groupie escort.

R: Jason gets drunk and makes stupid comments. I don't think that . . .

A: No, he said it on national television.

R: He did not!

A: He did. He was on *The View* two days ago. He was on *Howard Stern*. On *Geraldo*. Geraldo was ripping him apart. Whoopi Goldberg was ripping him apart. Every single media channel known to man. He was on *20/20*. He was talking about Ashley Dupré, who worked under the name of Victoria, and he said that she had the best pussy in town. He actually said that on *Howard Stern*.

Jason actually was close with two guys who had been cops. One of the guys had a friend who was the desk sergeant at Manhattan South who did all the busts for prostitution on the task force. So Jason would get girls—hypothetically, like Julie, I'm just giving you a name, who worked for multiple agencies. He'd befriend her, make her feel like she was really special to him, go shopping and buy her shoes. Treat her like she was his superstar. Then he would pump her for information. The girls would end up giving him credit card slips, the private phone numbers for the agencies, the setup for how it's done, how the apartments are set up. That motherfucker would put it all together and then hand it to that cop friend. His friend would come in, blow coke, and see a couple of girls for free, take the information and give it to the desk sergeant at the task force.

The next thing you know, remember Jeannine from American Beauty? Jet from Tower? All these people got taken down because of Jason Itzler. He went through the whole industry. He tried this shit with me. But I knew from an insider what was going down.

I have an ex-boyfriend. He's someone nobody fucks with. Get my drift? He's the guy who, you hear his name, no matter who you are . . . Put it this way, he was at Gotti's funeral. He dated Victoria Gotti. He's one of the most well-known guys . . .

R: Say that again?

A: OK, my ex-boyfriend, who I dated for three years. He looked out for me a lot. He's the guy, he's on television a lot; he's very well-known and he's very powerful on two sides of the coin. His best friend was chief director of the FBI for the entire country. When Itzler started shaking people down, he tried to shake me. Itzler called me up and said, "You need to shut down, or else I'm going to shut you down." I said, "Oh, really, motherfucker? Let's see what happens when my friend fucks up your face. Try to understand, you have an electronic bracelet on your ankle, right? You could go back."

You know he was arrested for drug dealing? Three thousand Ecstasy pills. [Itzler was sentenced to] a year and a half. He ratted out the Colombian drug cartel down in Miami because, before he came to New York, he was in Miami in the 900-number business. He was the number one guy in Florida, or so he alleges. There was another guy who was his competitor. I for one did not shut down. Itzler was partners with one of the Colombians. You know how these guys do? The Colombian necktie. The guy says he wants to close him down. A couple of months later he disappeared. They found him and his girlfriend decapitated in the trunk of their car. Out in the swamps, the Everglades. And suddenly Jason left town. He came to New York. He got on a plane to Amsterdam. You can go online and look at his parole record. He got a year and a half for international drug trafficking of 2,800 Ecstasy pills.

R: That's incredible!

A: Jason Itzler threatened me years ago, when I had a company with a different name. I got in a big pissing match with him. I said, "Listen, fuckface, you want to play the game?" I said, "You have an ankle bracelet, motherfucker." I picked up the phone and called my guy. My guy sent two guys down to [Jason's] office to make it very clear to him. When my guy spoke to his guy, he got it. That's why I was the only one who never went to jail when Jason was turning in all the names to Vice. There were eleven agencies busted in four months. That was all because of Jason. He went through the back of *New York* magazine, and all the agencies. He was meeting girls who worked for these agencies. And getting all the information and giving it to Vice. They'd go right in and close them down. He didn't do it with me. One, I didn't use credit cards. And two, I think my people made him very nervous.

Jason's guys thought they were pretty tough. But my guys were not the type of guys they wanted to bother. Jason did threaten me. But he never bothered me again.

Jason, the day he gets arrested, he gets out the next day. You don't think that's kind of coincidental? Now you see why I kept my distance from everybody. I'm paranoid about everyone I hire. It's craziness . . .

[Anna's sister] Elizabeth is just chilling out. She was worried about you. She said, "Please tell her not to be scared." When the storm blows over, she said you'll be on our list. Here's my new number: ———.

R: She's so sweet.

A: She's a nice lady. Her heart is good. She's very patient. So that's the latest gossip. Remember American Beauty and Femme Desire? They all got busted because of Jason. He was getting info from all these girls. He has his business up again. It's called DNA Diamonds. He's fucking running it.

R: It's pretty clever.

A: No, it's not pretty clever! Because he cannot control himself, his mouth, and his inability to not promote himself. He cannot be across from you: he has to be "I'm number one. I'm the biggest and the best." He's on all these radio and TV shows, telling everybody. They flew him to California. He was on *Geraldo.* I've never seen anything like this. He was on Channel 7; Channel 5; he was on CNN. He was on *Anderson Cooper* talking about Ashley Dupré. Do you even know that Ashley Dupré was with the Victoria's Agency? And just so everybody knows, she had a special thing to market: "she had the most beautiful pussy in New York."

R: Oh, really?

A: That's what he was saying on *Howard Stern.* It was just gross.

Anyway, I'm going to be honest: I don't think Kristin is going to mention your name. You're so far removed [from working for Kristin in the recent past]. I think she's going to be thinking about girls from the last six months. Do you know there're girls turning themselves in, like you thought you wanted to do? I told you that was a mistake. I knew girls were going to get scared, like you were feeling . . .

R: That's why I wanted to talk to you. Like, what am I supposed to do?

A: You go on with your life. You wait. Somebody shows up, you say, "I need an attorney." I'll be more than happy to come to the station with my attorney. I don't think they're going to look into you. My gut tells me you're safe. They're going to look at the last six months because it's more of an active time to nail her. It's so hard to track people down from a couple of years ago.

R: Jessica?

A: Yes, she would advertise. I hope you're sleeping a little better. I swear, if you need a place to stay—if it comes to that—you can come to my place. I have a two-bedroom. It's five hours from New York City by bus. It's not a big deal. I'm in a really nice area.

R: Oh, really?

A: It's nice. So if it gets crazy . . .

But about the media: if you really feel you'll get a knock at the door, and your name's going to come out, you will call me, right? Because I think I might be able to keep your name out of the papers.

R: Absolutely.

A: That would be my biggest concern if I were you. Forget the police. They're not going to arrest you on something you may or may not have done, going back two years ago. So the only thing you really have to worry about is the media. I think that's your biggest fear. Right?

R: Having my name in the papers is a major concern.

A: [Chuckles.] OK, one of my best friends is the chief editor there. The head editor. One of my very closest friends. You understand? I've never asked for a favor, other than my daughter. They were giving out student internships for the summer. That's the only thing I've ever asked, and I've known him for fourteen years. And, no, he's not a client, but, yes, he knows what I used to do. Put it this way: they've gotten a couple of their biggest stories from me, ever. And it was nothing to do with the adult industry. Do you remember the sultan of Brunei?

R: I can't recall.

A: That's how I started my business. I used to send the girls to Brunei.

R: Oh, wow.

A: I stopped booking them because I learned a lot of weird shit was going on there. A few years later, there was a huge scandal. Miss America—Shannon Something. Mamaroneck? [Marketic.] Allegedly she was sent over there and they tried to hold her hostage.

All the girls were totally gorgeous. They submit to HIV testing as soon as they arrive. They have a clinic. You fly into the private airport and they take you right to the clinic. They do all your blood work before you get sent to the harem. They do, honestly. She sued them for an undisclosed amount, and they wanted media coverage. An attorney who was co-counsel with the attorney on record knew that I was friends with the editor and said, "Can you get it into the paper?" I said, "Sure." It was a huge story for the [*New York Post*]. I've given them a couple of big stories that are not related to the sex industry here. I won't do the sex industry here because I think it's bad karma.

R: It *is* bad karma.

A: I was speaking to my friend who's a DA, and I said, "What do you think they're going to do with [Kristin's] case?" He tried to get an attorney's number for you. And who better to ask than one of the DAs? [Laughter.]

I know that you feel you're trapped in this world and you can't share it with many people . . .

R: That's the problem, you can't talk to anybody about it. Who can you talk to?

A: I'm here. I don't know if we're all just paranoid. Don't be scared to call anytime.

Call anytime? If only Anna knew.

going undercover

The assistant district attorney's office couldn't believe the information I provided in my first wiretap. But my work was far from over. It was clear to them I was an invaluable asset, and so they encouraged me to keep on working for Anna as a call girl. It was like the Wild West. They wanted me to keep breaking the law so they could get more information.

I highly doubt District Attorney Morgenthau was aware of the ADA's shenanigans. The ADA told me to work in order to garner information for him, and then turn over to his office the money and any gifts that clients gave me. I actually did this. God knows if somebody pocketed the money. Technically, this ADA was my pimp. It was like sex slavery at the behest of the Manhattan District Attorney's Office. This cowboy still has a job in law enforcement, in another state, at an even higher level.

Obviously, if I did this with every client I saw, I would have been broke, so I didn't tell him about everybody.

Anna continued to hook me up. One of my heavy hitters at the time was Brent. Brent was a complete sicko, but money was tighter than ever and I was compromising myself in ways I never thought possible. But if Brent wanted to see me twice in one week, I was $20,000 richer by Friday.

They weren't all bad. I had one client, an Asian billionaire who preferred to be called Henri, who was incredibly generous and easygoing. Henri was living in New York for about a year to sort out some banking problems, and his wife stayed back in their home country with the children. Henri had to have companionship, so he would have his chauffeur come pick me up in his Bentley. It was a bit awkward because his driver, John, was an off-duty cop, my client revealed with a chuckle. One night, John picked me up, and as we got stuck in a midtown logjam, I decided to break the barrier of silence. I didn't know if he would respond or not, but I asked him about himself and chatted amiably. But surely he knew what was going on.

Having someone who works as a police officer during the day drive me around, knowing full well that I was an escort, was not a comforting feeling. In fact, I was nervous each time I saw him. Henri always laughed at me and said, "If you pay those guys enough, they will do anything." That wasn't true, and I knew it. John needed the money to help pay for child support and was currently in the middle of a custody battle. Bingo! Right then I felt his pain and understood why he would take the demeaning commands from Henri and work ridiculous hours, only to wake up and go and be one of New York's Finest. A lot of police think prostitution is a BS crime and a waste of their time. I never told John why I did what I did, of course, and he probably did judge me, but for that night during the drive, we were not driver and escort. We were just John and Ashley.

Later that evening I told Henri that he had a wonderful driver and that I thought he was very kind. "Kind?" he asked. "What do you mean, kind? How would you know that? Did he talk to you?" I froze. A stream of thoughts and scenarios went through my head. Why was he so upset? All of a sudden I was nervous for John and his job, so I quickly said, "No, of course not. He is just a very good driver and always makes sure I know how far away we are from you when you are not with me in the car. You know how much I can't stand to be away from you and wait all by myself in the backseat." I put on my pouty face and cozied up to him so as to reassure him that there was nothing to worry about. Henri could be the biggest baby. After that, he refused to go out for the evening, so we stayed in, even though he had made special dinner plans with clients. He called his secretary at home and screamed at her to call them all and cancel. This was going to be a long night, and I was going to have my work cut out for me. Tonight wasn't about me. Tonight I had made a mistake, and it was talking to the driver and telling Henri. Now, I had to make him forget about it. It was time to "flip the switch," go into high gear, and make sure John didn't lose his job.

The next time John picked me up, I said hello to him with a smile you couldn't miss. He didn't respond. We rode in absolute silence all the way from downtown to a riverside skyscraper where Henri had an apartment so high up, you couldn't get cell phone service. We literally looked down on the clouds that drifted past the Citigroup Center and the Chrysler Building, twinkling like bling. He still had his job, but he never spoke to me again.

What Henri loved to do—besides have sex, of course—was watch college football when Stanford was playing. Perhaps he was an alumnus. He liked to uncork a pricey bottle of wine from his collection at every touchdown, and I remember we savored a bottle of Romanée-Conti and another of Pétrus during one game, which Stanford won. It put him in a particularly energetic mood in bed.

There was one client, François, whom I grew so close to that he tried to get me to leave the business and just be with him. He was the CEO of a European fashion company, and when he had business with the store executives in New York, he would come and stay at the Pierre and see me. I would stay with him for two or three days, and he would take me to Per Se, Le Bernardin, or La Grenouille. We might go to a concert at Carnegie Hall or Lincoln Center, if he had time.

For François, I dressed in Narciso Rodriguez, Marc Jacobs, and, of course, designers working for him. He expected the best. He was the most solicitous of lovers, always making sure my needs were taken care of. But sometimes we just talked. He was sad, because he had gotten a high-priced call girl in Europe pregnant and his wife found out and took his kids away from him. Unlike the others, when he was sad, he would cry and cry. Most nights he would cry himself to sleep and I would hold him. It truly was hard to tell if he was crying because he had been caught or because he was about to pay hefty sums of money to both his estranged wife and the girl he had gotten pregnant. What I did know for sure was that he was inconsolable about the loss of time with his children. François was feeling the pain of his actions brutally: not seeing his kids just tore his heart up. It is an unbelievable sight to see such a powerful figure in any industry be brought to his knees, but it reminds me that we are all human and that in the end family is the most important thing.

To be forced apart from one's child was something I understood all too well, and he wanted me with him all the time when he was in town because he felt I took care of him. I empathized, but I never told him of my dear sweet little girl, who had been ripped away from my life. His tears might as well have been mine, and that was our connection, even if he never knew it. Unbelievably, after all the pain he put himself and his family through due to his mistake, it didn't stop François from continuing to see hookers.

Meanwhile, my custody case slogged on, and my daughter was still languishing at her father's house in the care of various nannies.

Once, I was on the Upper West Side, and I saw Isabella across the street with two complete strangers. I froze. At the first hearing, the judge had ordered that I wasn't allowed to talk to her in between visits. If I violated that, my visits would be rescinded.

She was riding an electric pony outside a novelty store. I learned later that they were the parents of Isabella's stepmother. I couldn't call out to her; I couldn't go hug her; I could only stand there crying on the other side of the street and watch my own daughter from afar. It was the hardest thing I've ever done in my life.

I was more determined than ever to get my daughter back.

· · ·

The ADA wanted me to go after Anna's moneyman, Jonas Gayer. Gayer was a Russian émigré by way of Poland and Belgium who had been high up in the IRS before he got into a little trouble with the law. He was arrested in 1989 and accused of engineering a $10 million tax scheme for a Brooklyn trucking company. Andrew Maloney, the U.S. attorney for the Eastern District who later prosecuted John Gotti, said Jonas's scheme was "the largest evasion-of-payment scheme of its kind" ever attempted in the United States. Yet Jonas never served any prison time.

Now, with his knowledge of how to slide in and out of IRS loopholes, Jonas had a big accounting practice, and Anna was among his clients.

Bearing some resemblance to a weasel, he nevertheless got to have sex with me courtesy of Anna. I was his "Jonas Bonus" after he completed a particularly sticky bit of business for her. Anna paid me for my services, but he never had to pay her. He asked to see me quite regularly. I think he loved me a little bit. He thought his true calling was to be an artist, and he would give me seascapes he painted in acrylics and oils out at his country house on Shelter Island.

The early arrest had apparently not put a crimp in his wealth-building activities, since he also had a posh apartment on Beekman Place. His website boasts that his artwork "has been influenced by the exquisite views of Shelter Island and the busy life he leads in New York City as a tax advisor." Busy indeed.

The DA's investigators wanted me to visit Jonas at his accounting office and see what I could get out of him about Anna. The first trip would be simple, just a visit to establish contact independent of Anna and also to say that I needed advice about my own cash that I had stockpiled.

They gave me what was essentially a script of what I was supposed to say. They were lines like "Jonas, I have too much cash—like, $250,000. Should I invest it or launder it or what?"

Good Lord.

"That will never work," I said. "I can't go in and say these things!"

My escort persona, Ashley, would never even broach the topic. It would be completely out of character. Jonas had never talked to me about business before. And I had never asked him for business advice. They wanted too much too soon, and they were going to blow it. I knew how to get what they wanted, but they would have to do it my way.

"How am I supposed to get Jonas to help me launder my money when Anna knows exactly how much I make?" This conversation had taken place at least a few times, and they needed to understand it was the key element to the whole operation. I asked, "I'm supposed to show up with an extra quarter of a million dollars, when she knows that with my legal bills I couldn't have accumulated that much? She expects me to tell her everything. How do I know he's not going to tell her?" These were the arguments, plans, and ideas we would discuss for days, until they finally gave in and decided to trust me. They had to let me do it my way. In order for me to make sure Jonas would not say a word to Anna, I had to make him feel obligated to me personally and afraid of her. Only a woman who is trying desperately to hide money and work undercover knows how to do that. No ADA with a scripted dialogue was going to make that happen. I knew I could do it, and they were starting to see that I was getting them what they needed. They wanted to know where Anna's money was. I knew I could get him to tell me.

I was to wear a wire.

The investigators brought in their tech guy, and he said, "OK, the wire will go around your waist and then up here," gingerly indicating my chest.

"Are you kidding me?" I nearly screamed. "Do you not understand that this is a client? It's not going to work to wire my body, because the very first thing he's going to do is feel me up. There's no safe place on my body to put a wire. I don't know where he's going to touch me. But when he does, it's over."

"It won't be a big deal. It's going to be a short meeting," said the ADA, rolling his eyes. He just didn't get it, and he obviously didn't care. Jonas couldn't keep his hands off of me. He'd discover any device immediately, and God knows what he would do to me when he did.

I looked away in despair, but then suddenly it dawned on me: they needed me. They couldn't do this without me. I had an intimate relationship with Anna Gristina's moneyman, and nobody else had that sort of access. I realized I could take control of the situation.

"You guys had better start thinking about Plan B," I said, "because I'm not going anywhere with that ridiculous idea."

I didn't have full confidence in their competence. Or at least I felt they weren't really thinking this through in terms of my safety. Jonas, who was Russian himself, associated with members of the Russian underworld in Brooklyn. What did they think would happen if he discovered I was wearing a wire? Would they be so cavalier if I was an undercover cop? I wondered. Is it the usual prejudice against escorts? She's a prostitute, a "whore," and therefore somehow not deserving of care? I didn't think they gave a damn about me.

I had to think for myself, but I had been doing that ever since I was a little girl. I snapped out of my pity party.

"Would it work if the transmitter was in my purse, hidden in the lining?" I asked.

The investigators looked at the techie.

"It could work if we could make an opening in the pocket-book," he said. "And if you kept it within six feet of him at all times. And you can't carry a cell phone or have any electronics on inside it. They would interfere with the frequency."

"No cell phone?" I exclaimed.

"Don't worry. If something goes wrong, we'll hear you through the transmitter," said the techie. "We'll be out on the street."

"What if Jonas discovers the transmitter and destroys it?" I asked.

"We'll storm in, don't worry," said the head detective.

I hesitated. Did I really trust these guys? I would have to.

"All right. I'll do it. But you're going to have to spend money on this bag. It can't be some twenty-dollar bag. Jonas knows what kinds of purses I carry."

So the ADA's office bought me a black Chanel bag. It cost over $1,000, but they had to do it.

the madam's moneyman

I called Jonas and I asked him if I could come over. In my most helpless-sounding voice, I told him I had a problem and just didn't know what to do. I needed his advice.

"Sure!" he said. Perhaps he was hoping for sex. We set up a time for the very next day.

I had never met him at his office before. I could barely sleep all night, playing it out in my mind. Instead of having a trained female cop go undercover as a hooker, they were getting me to do their surveillance for them. They were having me take a huge risk. Throughout the night I tossed and turned, wondering how on earth I would get the information out of Jonas in a way that he wouldn't tell Anna. It finally came to me at about five a.m.

How would I do it? By getting him to show me everything about Anna's hidden accounts. He'd never want me telling Anna that he'd shown me her private business. Then I would have something on him. If I could pull it off.

I rose and showered and put on really sexy jeans, a sky-blue silk blouse, Chanel pumps, and pearls. Jonas liked that look.

I was picked up a couple of hours later and driven downtown to Corruption headquarters to prep for the encounter with Jonas as best I could. I got to the conference room just outside the lead ADA's office, where the prosecutors, investigators, and techies had gathered. The techies seemed more on point than before. They had the Chanel bag all ready for me. I could barely see the opening where the recording device was hidden.

The ADA went over my instructions again. And yet again. He wanted to make sure I knew what I was doing. Slightly insulted, I said, "Frankly, I think I am more prepared for this than you guys are." If I did it their way, something very bad could happen to me. I had to take control of the situation.

"Jonas is going to expect me to act like Ashley. You know me as Rebecca, but he doesn't know my real name or even my real personality. I have to put on my little show and do what I get paid for. I get it.

"I'm going to tell him I have a lot of cash that I've stashed away in another place that will take a while to get back here, but I need his advice on what to do with it.

"I understand that the point is to establish a relationship with him without Anna knowing. I really do not think any of you realize how dangerous that part is for me. Anna knows how much money I make. If I start throwing around different numbers and Jonas tells her about it, she is going to know something is up, so I have to literally pull off an Academy Award–winning performance here and make Jonas realize that he cannot tell Anna that we are seeing one another behind her back. And I have to do it all within a few feet of this Chanel bag at all times, all the while heading off all Jonas's attempts to have sex with me on his desk.

"So, if you don't mind, I would like to go now, and I would like a little silence on the ride up so I can mentally prepare."

This would be the first of many trips in "the van." The van had tinted windows and both sides of it could open so I could hop in and out quickly no matter which side of the street it was on. They would make sure in these situations that there was always a female officer with us. Maybe it was standard procedure. I climbed in the back and sat quietly as we moved out and began weaving in and out of traffic headed uptown. I would call Jonas soon to set our meeting time and get him excited. My heart was beginning to beat faster. What if Jonas discovered the recording device? What if he figured out what I was up to?

The stress was overwhelming, and I knew that one wrong move and I was in serious trouble. They may be able to cover me today, but not after that. Anna would find out, and I would be screwed. Jonas was involved with some seriously dangerous people, as was Anna. Time for my phone call . . .

"Jonas, my love," I drawled. "Do you still have time for little old me?"

"Ashley, darling, get over here as soon as you can. I am waiting for you!" Jonas enthusiastically replied. *Excellent,* I thought.

He's in a good mood. "I'll be there in a little bit. I can't wait to see you. I've missed you. And I am excited to finally see all your artwork."

He laughed, and I could tell he was pleased. "You missed me? I love it. I bet we can do something about that when you get here, my sweet princess."

I could almost feel him smiling on the other end of the phone. "Kiss kiss, darling," I said with a smooch. "See you soon!"

The investigators wanted me to be very observant about the layout. "Take a mental photograph of where his desk is," they told me, "where the lamps are; the TV; where his computer is." They would need that information in advance to surreptitiously go in there and plant bugs quickly.

I rang the bell, and Jonas answered the door himself. He was so happy to see me. We'd always met in hotel rooms before. The very first thing he did was take my purse and set it down on his desk so he could pull me towards him. He started rubbing his hands over my body in exactly the places I told the techie he would.

"Mmmm . . . somebody's feeling frisky today," I teased as I wiggled away, casually picked up my purse, and moved towards his computer, pretending to be interested in a painting of a sunset that was similar to one he had given me. I saw his signature in the bottom right corner.

"Jonas, you didn't do this one, did you?" I squealed. "It's magnificent! It's not just yellow and orange and red—it's a dozen subtle shadings of each. I remember you telling me white is never white: if you really look at it, it's all grays and blues and greens."

I think he actually blushed. I placed my purse on the desk next to his computer. The TV was very loud, and I was worried that the transmitter mike wouldn't pick up what he said. *Judge Judy* was on, and the litigants were cursing at each other.

"Jonas, why do you watch these shows?"

"It's just background while I work," he said, zapping it off with the remote. "I don't need it now that you're here." He leered.

He came up behind me and gave me a wraparound hug.

"So what's up, bubby?" he said as he rubbed his groin on my backside.

I gently took him by the hand and sat him in his desk chair and then sat on his lap.

"Well, here's my situation," I said. "I have cash hidden back home in another state. I don't know what to do with it. I know there are laws where you can't just bring bags of money into a bank and deposit it without getting a suspicious-activity report filed on you from Homeland Security, right?"

"You're brainy as well as beautiful! But I knew that . . ." he said, rubbing my inner thigh.

"Well, should I bring it back to New York? Anna has always said that she trusts you and you're the one to go to if I ever need anything. Anna doesn't know how much money I have, so I'm trusting you now."

I slipped my fingers between the buttons of his shirt and gently rubbed circles on his chest.

"Can I trust you, baby?" I purred. "I don't want anyone knowing my business."

"Yes, yes, yes," he said, his breathing starting to be a bit labored.

You could see where his loyalties lay: he would get a lot more pleasure out of me than from Anna. He jumped right in.

"Here are your options," he said. "Your best option is real estate. You can buy it with cash. There's no Patriot Act rule requiring reporting cash over $12,000 when you buy property with it. You just have to pay different lawyers to sign off on LLCs."

"LL whats?" I asked, all wide-eyed.

"Limited liability companies. You set up shell companies. No one can figure out who the other owners are. It's a good investment. That's if you don't need to get to your money right away. If you do, you can put it in the bank. I can help you with that."

I nuzzled his neck and kept playing the stupid little girl to his financial genius.

"I don't understand how any of this works," I said in my cutest Southern drawl. "Anna just seems so savvy about money."

"That's because she has me, baby," he crowed.

"Well, what do you do for her? Can you show me?" I asked, grazing my hand back and forth over his fly. He leaned back his head and smiled, closing his eyes and giving a little moan.

"Can you give me a peek at her accounts?" I said with a naughty smile just before I started nibbling the lobe of his ear, which was his weak spot.

"Mmmmmm . . . I'd rather peek at your accounts, doll," he chuckled. But then he typed something on his keyboard, and up popped a spreadsheet.

On the screen in front of me was the name Anna Gristina, with a list of account numbers and the balance in each account. There were names of her LLCs with made-up names. I remember she'd once told me about these shell companies and that she thought it was funny to give them names that sounded like law firms, like "Fido, Rover & Schmidt." But then I saw a serious number. At the bottom was the total of Anna's portfolio. It was over $14 million.

Jonas explained the details of the different accounts, and I could see he was getting bored—and amorous.

"Let's get a room," he said, and clicked CLOSE.

from brooklyn russians
to beekman place
bankers

My handlers at the DA's office were pleased with me. But it was not enough for them. I would now have to actually go with Jonas and launder the money.

They had to request the cash. Law enforcement agencies have access to large amounts of cash seized from drug dealers and other criminals. It had to be approved by the big bosses. The cash had to be in nonsequential order. Some of it was in fifties and some in twenties. The bills were rubber-banded up, as if I had done it myself.

The following week, I brought about $100,000 of it in a Louis Vuitton book bag to Jonas's office. At least I could zip it closed.

Lord knows what would have happened if I had gotten mugged that day. Jonas peeked inside and then opened his top desk drawer. It was spread clear across with gold jewelry with real stones.

"You could always buy this," he said with a sly smile. "It belongs to Jocelyn Wildenstein. Her ex-husband gave it to her, and she's trying to unload it."

Jocelyn Wildenstein had had a very public divorce from wealthy art dealer Alec Wildenstein. She became famous for getting so much plastic surgery that she could no longer close her eyes all the way. *Vanity Fair* had called her "the Bride of Wildenstein." She had wanted to look like a lioness, apparently because Alec had found that sexy. I looked at the collection of solid-gold dog collars and leopard brooches with emeralds for eyes and shook my head. "Nice try, Jonas."

No, we were going to have to deal with the Russians. The ones who had immigrated to Brooklyn neighborhoods like Brighton Beach and Sea Gate and made millions in one generation by whatever means necessary. They had built ostentatious mansions filling entire city lots where small vinyl-sided split-levels once stood. We hopped in Jonas's Lexus and drove past these monuments to money all the way to Coney Island, where the bitter winter wind kept the streets empty. We parked on Surf Avenue outside the Coney Island Circus Sideshow, where a mural showed a beautiful tattooed and pierced woman named Insectavora eating a giant bug. (And people denigrate what *I* do for a living . . .)

Soon a Maybach drove up. Adrenaline shot through my body, but I quickly memorized the plate numbers. It had tinted windows, and the driver indicated that he wanted us to get in the backseat. My fear level was spiking. I looked at Jonas and he nodded, opening the door for me.

Inside, we found two older men in overcoats and fedoras. No introductions were made. Jonas told me to hand over the bag. I passed the Louis Vuitton over to one of the old men, and he opened it in a routine way and had no visible reaction to the sight of tens of thousands of dollars' worth of rolled-up bills. He pulled out a fifty and rubbed his thumb over Ulysses S. Grant's face. Then he held it up to the light, no doubt looking for Grant's second, hidden portrait or the vertical stripe that read USA FIFTY. He pulled out a twenty and subjected it to the same process, then took out a small gold magnifying glass on a watch fob to examine another fifty, which must have passed muster. He gave a curt nod to the other old man and said something in Russian.

That one took out a checkbook and asked in accented English, "What's the name?" He then signed about ten checks alternately to me and to "Cash." They had already been filled out in varying amounts up to $10,000 but totaling $80,000. They took 20 percent, Jonas had warned, and of course he would take his cut. That was the deal. They handed the checks to him, and he handed them to me, and I saw that the imprint was for an antiques business in Manhattan. A brilliant ploy: I could have sold them my aunt Tilly's silver, for all Uncle Sam knew.

"I hope you don't mind if I count mine too," I dared to say.

There was a pause, and then Jonas burst into laughter, and so did they. "I told you she was like us," said Jonas.

I tried to engage them in chitchat about antiques, but it was obvious they knew nothing about them. The meeting was over. They didn't leer; they didn't judge. Oddly enough, there was a feeling of respect. Here was another person beating the government system.

"You can keep the bag!" I said over my shoulder as we exited. More guffaws. It had almost been friendly. But I shudder to think what would have happened if they had discovered my recorder.

Jonas and I got back into his car and headed back to Manhattan. As we pulled out I noticed another van make the turn right after us. The damn investigators, who should have known better. I was pissed. These guys needed to fall back. They were too close, and it was going to get me killed. My adrenaline level shot up again, and I hoped Jonas didn't notice.

Jonas said we couldn't launder all the money with his Russian friends. I would have to start banking money, and he had a friend who was head of a local bank branch who would do him the favor.

He told me to bring another bag over to his office, this time with $50,000 in it. Another detective gave me a bag of twenties for that amount in nonsequential order, rolled up in rubber bands.

"Where do you get all this?" I asked him.

"This batch? A guy running guns up from your neck of the woods," he said.

"Quite a profitable business," I said.

"Until you're caught," he said.

I thought with wonder and amazement about the NYPD detectives making $48,000 a year who go undercover and risk their lives and are out there seizing buckets of cash from sleazebags like it's only so much paper—and they don't take a bit of it. What integrity they have! And now the money was being put to use, hopefully for the good.

They installed a transmitter in another purse, this time a

shoulder bag, since I would be walking with Jonas. And he knew I didn't repeat bags very often.

"You can talk with the purse on," the detective told me. "We'll be parked in a van outside. You can't hear us, but we can hear you. We'll also have people posted around on the street if you get into trouble. We will help you. Don't worry."

I *was* worried.

When I walked into Jonas's office, he hugged me and said, "Congratulations, beautiful! You're now the president of Ashley Enterprises Inc." He had set up a corporation for me in Delaware.

"Oh, really?" I said, smiling. "What are my products?"

"Beauty and delight," he said, giving my ass a squeeze. "Whatever you want. We'll celebrate later, but right now, let's go see my friend at the bank."

We left the very exclusive Beekman and walked to a busier part of the Upper East Side and turned into a corner bank.

Jonas had some sort of relationship with the branch manager; he'd probably brought him all sorts of business. He jumped up at the sight of Jonas and greeted us warmly. After the introductions, we went into his glass office.

"She's in the nightclub business," Jonas ventured. "She works the door, and you'd be amazed at how much people will give her to get in. It's personal gifts, it's not wages, and I don't see why we have to raise the attention of the IRS about it."

Apparently, neither did the branch manager. "How much does she have?" he asked.

"Today, $50,000," said Jonas.

The bank manager raised his eyebrows.

"Oh, it's a very exclusive club," Jonas said. "And she's a very good saver. She'll be making more deposits in the future, maybe not as big, but every week. She's starting a business; here are the documents. She wants to start two commercial accounts for the business to break it up a little."

The manager took out his reading glasses and looked over the papers. He then turned to his computer and started cautiously typing, looking at me every so often over the glasses. He picked up the phone, and cold fear shot through me—I thought he was calling security—until he said, "Miss Ruiz, could you tell Mr. Vitale that our meeting has to be pushed back thirty minutes? Thank you.

"I'll handle that myself," he said to me, indicating the bag of cash, which I handed him. "Do you want to wait while our machines verify the amount?"

"No, no, we trust you, Robert," said Jonas, who then smiled and put his arm around my waist. "Besides, we have reservations." *We do?* I thought. *All the cops outside don't know that.* Perhaps Jonas was just showing off to the other fifty-something man.

"I'll let you know if there's a discrepancy," said the banker, looking piercingly into my eyes. He then stood up and extended his hand. "Welcome to our bank, Ms. Kade."

"Let's celebrate, starting with lunch," said Jonas as he put his arm around me and steered me down the block to a restaurant— his friend's place. This was not part of the plan. When we walked out, I saw a couple of detectives in two different places on the block. One was across the street, while another was at the newsstand by the bank. They never looked up, and I never looked at them, but we were all very much aware of one another and that the plans had changed. They had heard the whole exchange. Jonas and I were not supposed to go to lunch, but I felt that rushing off would look bad, so I decided to go with it and hope that it was the right thing to do. We walked in, and at the sight of Jonas they began clearing the place. Man, you help people avoid paying taxes and you walk on a red carpet everywhere you go.

It was nearly three o'clock, but there were still a few people lingering over their cappuccinos.

"I'm terribly sorry," I heard one waiter say. "But we must prepare the restaurant for a special party coming in. The owner will be happy to cover your dessert."

Assuaged, the people left, and Jonas and I had the entire restaurant to ourselves. The owner greeted Jonas heartily and said, "Mademoiselle, what do you desire? Don't even bother with the menu, the chef can make anything you want."

I just had a little French onion soup. I was too freaked out to eat.

"I really have to go, Jonas," I said. "I appreciate everything, but I have an appointment."

"Are you sure?" he said, looking surprised. He'd obviously expected sexual favors. "I could get us a room."

I had turned him down on the room each time and I was worried it was going to piss him off and that he would complain to Anna. I promised him next time we would plan for it to be part of our day and he definitely had some special attention coming his way as I reached under the table and teased him. It was enough to make him forget about the possibility of getting angry, and I felt as if I had dodged a bullet.

I looked at my watch. "Oh, no! Is it really four o'clock? I really must run, Jonas! Thanks for everything, and I'll call you tomorrow!"

I ran out the door and up the block, past the bank.

Now, I don't know if the bank manager had been standing at the window looking for me, but there he was, peering at me through the glass. And when he spotted me, he threw on his coat, ran out, and caught up with me.

"Miss Kade, I see you're walking in the same direction I am."

I had to think on my feet. I was supposed to meet the female detective just half a block up. We were already off schedule thanks to that stop at the restaurant, and I could actually see her up ahead. She took a right, where I was supposed to go. I couldn't follow her now. If I lost her, I was in trouble: I had no cell phone, no money, no keys, not even a Metro card. I didn't see the DA's van anywhere. The transmitter in my bag functioned best when I didn't have anything in there at all, so I had to reconnect with the detectives, and this bank manager could cause me to lose them. What was he up to?

"Can I get you a taxi?" he asked, narrowing his eyes a bit, and I started to get the feeling he didn't believe my story back at the bank.

"No, thank you, I feel like walking," I said.

"In those shoes?" he sneered, indicating my five-inchers. "You don't walk in those shoes."

"These little kitten heels?" I quipped. "These are my hiking boots."

"Ha. In that case, I'll walk you to where you're going," he said.

He's totally onto me, I thought. Maybe he was having second thoughts about our little business transaction earlier. Perhaps he was hitting on me. My mind raced, and I could not shake him. He was still following me after five, six, seven blocks along Madison Avenue. I hoped that the detectives were still getting transmissions through my purse. I started giving clues as to my location.

"Oh, I just *adore* how the Ralph Lauren shop decorates for the holidays, don't you?" I cooed, and then, a couple blocks further, "Mmmm . . . I would *love* a new Coach bag just like that one in the window, but I can't decide on a color," I said. "Did you know that Coach repairs bags free for life?"

I chattered inanely about shopping all the way down to Barney's while the banker fished around about my cash.

"That certainly is a lot of money for door tips," he said. "Do people really want to get into your club that badly?"

"Apparently so!" I blurted. "Oh, look, we're at Barney's. You know what? I think I might pick up a few things in here—intimate things, if you know what I mean," I said with a wink.

What was he going to do, follow me around as I purchased lace thongs? Whatever his suspicions were, whatever regrets he may have been having, there was nothing he could do about them now. He hailed a taxi and mournfully got in.

"Sure I can't give you a lift?" he asked.

"Shopping calls!" I sang out, and the taxi sped off.

Just then a female detective, my contact, emerged from Barney's. It had been a close call.

"Thank goodness!" I said as I grabbed her. "I thought I would never lose him! I think he is totally onto me. Never again are we doing it like that. You *cannot* leave me out there with no way of getting out of situations!" I was yelling at this point as she hurried me towards the van. I hopped in, furious and still terrified.

"Could you guys even hear me?" I screeched. "I was trying to talk and tell you where I was!"

"No, we couldn't hear anything," said one techie, his head-phones resting on his shoulders. "All of a sudden you were gone. We kept looking for you until we found you."

Fantastic, I thought. I could have been in serious danger in a car on its way out of town and these guys would not know how to find me.

"We would have found you with your transmitter eventually," said one cop.

"*Eventually?*" I yelled. "That's great. So as long as you can find my body *eventually*, I'm feeling better about the situation."

My anger did not subside as we headed back downtown to Corruption headquarters. I had a few choice words for the ADA in the debriefing.

Three days later, I got a bill from Jonas in the mail. He was probably mad that we hadn't had any sex after he'd done me such a big favor by setting me up at the bank.

Two days after that, on March 21, 2010, Jonas was arrested.

wearing a wire with
the madam

had admitted to prosecutors months before that Anna Gristina had procured me to perform sex acts in exchange for money—a lot of money—from men. I had lured Anna's moneyman, Jonas Gayer, into a meeting with the Russian money launderers. The DA's investigators had even taped it. I had gotten Jonas to show me her accounts, and I recorded him explaining how she hid her money, possibly as much as $14 million. Surely they now had enough evidence to arrest and convict Anna Gristina, if they were competent enough. I wanted to get my life back. But the prosecutors only wanted more.

They wanted me to wear a wire with the lawyer who seemed to have a special place in Anna's life. I'll call him Donald.

It was he who had advised her on investing in real estate. He introduced her to some of her richest clients.

For the lawyer's efforts, Anna gave him his choice of her girls. He chose me. I was the payoff. I had about six sessions like this over time.

The investigators in the Corruption Unit got very excited when they heard that this lawyer was my client. Apparently somebody else had tipped them off about him. I'm guessing Jonas was blabbing like Chatty Cathy after his arrest. Known as "John Doe" during the legal proceedings, Jonas was to testify before Judge Juan Merchan more than a dozen times. So investigators had their eye on this attorney. But they were going to have the same problem with him as with Jonas: his hands were going to be all over me if we had a scheduled liaison.

And then something incredible happened. Anna returned from Canada and wanted me to come to the East Seventy-Eighth Street place to meet and then go eat lunch. She said she wanted to discuss the business. Lately we had been discussing on the phone about her starting up new websites for a match-making site. It seemed harmless, and the ADA and detectives were thrilled at the opportunity to have me meet her face-to-face while wearing a wire. I was chilled with fright. But then I thought, *Maybe this is straight-up: she's paranoid and probably wants to get back out of town, so this will be a quick lunch.* Maybe she wanted me to manage some of the day-to-day tasks of operating the business—for a bigger stake and at increased risk, but I highly doubted this. I agreed to meet her the following week. What choice did I have?

This time the techies wanted me to wear the wire. "The audio from the recorder buried in the purse is simply not as good," said the lead detective. "We can't take any chances on this one, with both of them in the room talking."

On the appointed day, I was picked up and brought to Corruption. The DA's techies wired me up. The team drove me uptown in the surveillance van to East Seventy-Seventh Street, and I hopped out and walked the rest of the way to the apartment, where I thought only Anna was waiting for me. The detectives were in the van and in a couple of places out on East Seventy-Eighth. They had decided it was too risky to go inside. I don't know why it only occurred to me just as I was entering the building, but I realized that if things backfired and Anna wanted to hurt me, the cops wouldn't be able to get to me in time. I was on my own there.

I walked into the building and up the stairs to Anna's apartment, using my own key to enter. When I opened the door, I was stunned to see Anna sitting side by side with her attorney, Donald. He wasn't supposed to be there, and he most certainly would not go out in public with us to have lunch. He was rarely seen in public anywhere. I struggled to hold myself together and also listen to her. In my panic, my heart was racing, and I struggled to focus. I was Rebecca, then Ashley—no, wait, I was undercover Rebecca . . . no, I was absolutely confused . . . and then I snapped into place. I had a job to do. This is why the DA's office had me working for so long. I may have struggled internally, but in a mere moment I could completely pull off the performance of a lifetime and no one in that room had a clue I was scared or nervous. Not even the slightest suspicion.

Anna chatted amiably, but nothing concrete came up at first.

I tried to steer the conversation towards the business, but she was having none of it. It soon became clear what she wanted.

"Ashley, darling, Donald has been missing you *so much*," she said, practically cooing as he grinned. "He's been so nice to us, and I would like you to make him feel good today."

Anna wanted me to have a session with Donald right then! Maybe he had done her a real estate favor last week, maybe he was just horny, but it was payback time, and the reward was to be me. Donald sat there grinning.

Oh, God! I had wires running up to my breasts! I had a device on! I was dead! My mind raced. Should I tell them I was having my period? That I felt the flu coming on?

"Oh, Donald, there's *nothing* I'd love to do more," I said, reaching over and running my hand up his thigh. "But I have to go pick up Isabella early from school for her doctor's appointment." Donald was one of the few clients who knew I had a daughter.

"Can't her nanny do that?" Anna practically spit out.

"I *always* accompany her to her pediatrician, Anna, as I'm sure you do with your children," I said as I slowly started to rise and back out towards the door. "Let's set up a time so I can give you the proper attention you deserve."

"It doesn't have to be a long marathon," Donald pleaded in a last-ditch effort to get me to stay.

I unlocked the door, and they started to rise as Anna said, "Ashley, wait!"

I just yelled, "Gotta go!" from the hallway and I noticed my voice sounded unnaturally high.

All I could think about was getting to that van and getting that wire off, going downtown, being debriefed, and being taken home. I could barely breathe. This time was different. I knew if Anna and Donald had realized what I had been doing—well, I couldn't think about what would have happened. All I knew was that no one, no matter what they said, could have gotten to me quickly enough inside that apartment.

The investigators offered to drive me home, but I insisted on going alone. I had to get out of there and away from them. I called my sister as soon as I turned the corner.

"Hey. It's Rebecca."

"I know. How are you doing? How is Isabella?" she asked.

"She's fine, but I'm not doing too well. I wish I could come down there."

Bridget was silent.

"I just want this all to end."

"Rebecca, what did you think would happen when you got yourself wrapped up in that business?"

"I know, I know. I was just doing it for Isabella . . ."

"Remember the song, 'It's a long old road, but I'm gonna find the end.'"

"I hope so, Bridget. I . . . I just wanted to hear your voice. I needed to hear it. Tell me I'm going to be OK. I'm so scared."

"You are going to be OK. You are strong. And Isabella needs you. You told the truth, and that's all that matters. Be proud of that. OK? Keep me apprised of your situation. I need to know you are safe. Maybe we'll see you at Christmas?"

"OK. Sounds good. I love you."

"I love you too. Give Isabella hugs and kisses."

• • •

I couldn't even speak with my sister about what the DA was putting me through. I had to think for myself. And I decided that I was done with this. I didn't want any part of this any longer. There had been too many close calls. The more I gave the prosecutors, the more they wanted. They did not seem to care about me at all.

One day the detectives brought me down to Corruption and into the ADA's conference room, and the ADA started to say, "OK, next we want you to . . ." There was something presumptuous about his tone. He didn't ask me. He was telling me. I had been doing this for about two years now, and I had had enough.

I said "No" before he had even finished.

"What do you mean, 'No'?" he asked, startled. The other ADA and the investigators fairly whipped their heads in his direction.

"I think I need an attorney and I need protection," I said. "I've never been charged with anything, and you've been putting me into risky situations, including during client sessions, for too long."

The ADA stared at me, and his face was turning red. His visions of being the golden boy who brought down Manhattan's biggest madam were evaporating because I was going to lawyer up. Perhaps he should have treated me better.

"You can hire one," he blurted out.

"No, I have a right to a public defender," I said, looking him right in the eye. "And you're going to get me one."

He stormed out of the room and, for all I know, out of the Manhattan district attorney's office. I never heard from him again, and now he is working as an assistant U.S. attorney. I wish them luck with that cowboy.

I was still working for Anna as if nothing had happened. Unless somebody suddenly wanted to give me an investment banking job, there was no way I could make that kind of money for my fight, which raged on in Family Court. I continued to have supervised visits with my daughter. I could focus on school again, and my grades were improving. I was returning to normal. I felt I had gotten my life back.

And then, eleven months later, I received a call from the new ADA on the case. They had not given up on bringing Anna down. My whole feeling of well-being instantly collapsed. Why? Why were they doing this? Weren't there terrorists and murderers and Wall Street cheats to go after? What did Anna Gristina do, really? Facilitate paid sex between consenting adults? As they say in Nevada, where prostitution is legal: "If it doesn't scare the horses, who cares?"

The ADA told me I had to come back down to Corruption headquarters.

"I'm not coming in," I said, "until I have an attorney."

"No problem," he said. He soon arranged for the court to assign me a lawyer named Seema Iyer. Seema called me and we met in her office, where I sat and told her my entire story. She was flabbergasted. She knew the first ADA well, and couldn't believe how he had treated me.

She made big trouble and said I could bring a lawsuit against the city if I wanted to, because it was patently illegal for them to make me continue working in an illegal business. Not to mention hypocritical.

The new ADA said that all the work I did under the first ADA was thrown out, because it would be inadmissible in court. I was given all this information from my attorney, who had a conversation with him. I never went in to speak with him or meet him. My attorney completely shielded me from that office. It was a different experience from what I had gone through on my own prior to that. What's more, the new ADA told me that many documents were missing, including some of mine. I would have to start all over again, he said.

"In fact, Ms. Kade, we have evidence now to charge you on three different counts of prostitution and could do so at anytime," the ADA said. It was blackmail. I felt like he was trying to intimidate me into going back to work for them under these threats. I stood my ground.

"You could plead to a lesser charge," my lawyer told me.

"I'm not pleading to crap!" I yelled.

I had made copies of every letter, kept the statements of every fake bank account, saved every e-mail with instructions from the DA's office. (And still have them.) Not only that, but even as they were putting wires on me, I had been recording *them*. That's right: I had recorded the proceedings of every meeting and phone call on my little recorder. My job was done: if they'd messed up, they could find a new girl to risk her life for them. I would fight them, and my attorney was ready.

So they simply took her off my case. They assigned me a new public defender. It was all perfectly legal. And he happened to have worked in the DA's office prior to going into private practice. He didn't pursue any action against them, but the message had been sent. No one ever threatened me with charges again; in fact, I didn't hear from this ADA again.

gristina goes down

On July 19, 2011, Anna was having lunch with a wealthy man she had recently met, along with Jaynie Mae Baker, an alluring toffee-haired thirty-year-old. Jaynie Mae had once donned a bikini and a studded stretch halter with choker collar as a World Wrestling Entertainment (WWE) Raw Diva Search finalist, telling judges she was a "saucy little sushi roll." She was pretty and slender enough to work for Anna as an escort, but she didn't, as far as I knew. I never worked with her, anyway.

Jaynie Mae had a wealthy boyfriend, Wall Street investment banker Marcus Laun. And she had seen how much money there was to be made with a business like VIP Life, where she was the recruiting director. Like Anna, VIP Life founder Lisa Clampitt hooked up wealthy men with "beautiful and sophisticated" young women—for a hefty fee. But what Clampitt does is completely aboveboard in the eyes of the law: it's a relationship matchmaking service, Clampitt says on her VIP Life website, between "beautiful, sophisticated women" and men "who have all achieved professional success: physicians, attorneys, CEOs, entertainment industry professionals, etc., with quality lifestyles." Women pay nothing; men pay a large fee to date them—enough so that Clampitt allows only thirty men to be part of her service at any one time. Whether they have sex is their business; Clampitt's already been paid just for the introduction.

Anna wanted in on a business like this, without all the complications and risk of prostitution. Who knew how to cater to the desires of wealthy men better than she? Anna wanted to go legit, and Jaynie Mae knew the, um, ins and outs. They would be partners, and their luncheon companion was a potential investor.

Or so they thought. Today, Jaynie Mae's luncheon partner was interested in something else: a ménage a trois. "I'm looking for a little adventure," he said coyly. "Please corrupt me."

Jaynie Mae wasn't into that, but Anna could connect him with two young women who'd be only too happy to oblige: elegant blue-eyed brunette Catherine DeVries, and a blond design student from Birmingham, England, with a Scottish first name: Mhairiangela "Maz" Bottone. How much? Two for the price of one: $2,000 in cash for one hour. An appointment was set six days later at the apartment Anna kept for such purposes in an unassuming five-story brick building at 304 East Seventy-Eighth Street.

Catherine and Maz were there waiting for their gentleman

caller when he arrived on the dot. The threesome repaired to the bedroom. The girls stripped down to their lingerie, but the businessman settled into an easy chair at the foot of the bed and started telling them what to do. He just wanted to watch, he said. His requests got dirtier and dirtier, and finally the hour was up and they were finished. The voyeur handed the naked women $2,000. I don't know if his thank-you was recorded by the video camera, which caught the whole show. But his entire conversation at lunch with Anna and Jaynie Mae was. The "businessman" was a cop.

But Manhattan district attorney Cyrus Vance Jr. didn't have DeVries and Bottone arrested until seven months later. He didn't want to tip off Anna, who was a Scotland native with an apartment in Canada and possible millions at her disposal and therefore a flight risk. After five years he wanted the case to be rock-solid.

Vance had just taken office the year before, after DA Robert Morgenthau retired in 2009. Morgenthau had anointed Vance, the son of JFK's secretary of the Army and Jimmy Carter's secretary of state but who had established a career out of his father's shadow in Seattle, with his endorsement. Vance won in a landslide with 91 percent of the vote, and he set about doing things differently.

Vance had two new no-nonsense prosecutors on the Anna Gristina case: ADA Charles (Charlie) Linehan and ADA Elizabeth Roper. They both had reputations for being tough and following the straight and narrow. When they were brought in on the case, at some point Charlie called me and asked if I would come in so he could speak with me. I was so sad. I thought this Anna stuff was over. He promised that he only wanted to talk and we agreed that because it was merely a conversation, a lawyer was not needed on my part. He kept his end of the deal. At least the rogue behavior of past ADAs was over. Linehan wasn't even having any of the hooker jokes one particular detective used to crack in my presence. This grinning jackass seemed to have an unlimited store of jokes with "ho" in the punch line. He tried it once, and Charlie shot him a look that ended them once and for all. Charlie seemed like he would be more protective of me than his predecessors.

Anna and Jaynie Mae went on to meet and plan their venture, unaware that they were being watched. In October they co-hosted a benefit for the Shelby Shelter, an Allen, Texas, pet-rescue outfit run by Jaynie Mae's equally pretty sister Jessica. They held it at the West Village nightclub 49 Grove, owned by lady-loving Hamptons restaurateur Aram Sabet. Whether Anna genuinely loved animals or whether she needed a "gentleman farmer" tax break, she took in rescued dogs and potbellied pigs at her two-hundred-acre spread in Monroe, New York, in upstate Orange County. This was up her alley, and she and Jaynie Mae jointly publicized it on Facebook.

Anna was becoming increasingly paranoid. I hadn't been working for her for a while, but she called me and asked me to see an old client. I agreed because I knew he was safe and I wouldn't be arrested, and also I felt it was her way of checking to see if she could trust me. My rationale was if I took the job, she would not think I had any connection to law enforcement. What's more, I was going to be with what I called a no-sex client and a big tipper, so I gave in.

Anna also asked me to check the East Seventy-Eighth Street apartment for a plumbing problem, and when I got there she was inside. I was startled and a little nervous, wondering if it was a setup. But Anna had simply forgotten that she had asked me to check it, which wasn't like her—she was usually so on top of things. Anna looked totally freaked out. She was either wearing a wig or had gotten her hair cut short and dyed. She was in sweats and a hoodie, which she had pulled over her head even inside the apartment, and there was also a man with her I had never seen before. I think the detectives watching her knew they'd have to make their move soon, before she fled to her place in Montreal.

Meanwhile Jonas Gayer, known as "John Doe," was talking like a tattletale. He even gave my name up. Anna, who had in the past been so careful, and Jaynie Mae had not so brilliantly friended Jonas on Facebook and Twitter. When the *New York Post* asked him about that later, Jonas was so loquacious, he volunteered that he knew Anna through "a mutual friend . . . Bruno Jamais . . . a restaurant owner." I'm sure the famous chi-chi chef of the Restaurant Club appreciated that little advertisement.

I did testify in judge's chambers. But I had my limits. I never named names when it came to clients. I had too many strong feelings for them, however complex. It's a free country, and my clients have made plenty of money in it. If they wanted to spend it on sex and I was willing to give it, that was our business. I did testify that there was one client who made a request to obtain a young boy. But mostly I had given prosecutors some of the evidence they needed to bring down the "Millionaire Madam," who at fifteen years had the longest-running high-class call-girl agency in modern New York City history. After a five-year investigation, it would be up to Linehan and Roper of the Manhattan DA's Corruption Unit to prove it in court.

Yet on the morning of February 22, 2012, a grand jury

indicted Anna on just one single felony charge of promoting prostitution, based on the undercover cop's testimony about the girl-on-girl action the previous July. Jaynie Mae was also indicted on a felony procuring charge. Catherine DeVries and Maz Bottone were each indicted on one count of prostitution, a misdemeanor; DeVries was arrested on February 27; cops busted Bottone four days later on March 2. Both started cooperating immediately, Linehan told Judge Merchan. They were released without bail.

Investigators knew on the day she'd been indicted that Anna was to meet with David S. Walker, a financial adviser at Morgan Stanley, to talk to him about investing in her high-end relationship service. Anna was tailed as she went up to Walker's office for the meeting at Morgan Stanley headquarters in Times Square. When she reemerged, cops arrested her on the sidewalk. Anna thought she was being kidnapped and screamed out to passersby, "Please! Somebody! Call 911!"

Meanwhile, Walker had some explaining to do to Morgan Stanley honchos once it broke in the press that it was he who had had the "Millionaire Madam" up to their offices. He was never charged with any crime, and he told his superiors at Morgan Stanley that he had previously met Anna socially and just wanted to hear her business plan. Nevertheless, top execs would suspend him with pay until Anna's trial was over.

Anna was brought to her February 23 arraignment in cuffs, where she pled not guilty to her one charge of promoting prostitution. It was the first time, after being in the sex business for fifteen years as Anna Scotland, that she had ever been charged with a crime. Yet Judge Juan Merchan set her bail at an eye-popping $2 million bond, or $1 million in cash, which Anna couldn't—or wouldn't—make. Charlie Linehan had argued that Anna's wealthy clients, and perhaps Anna herself, had millions to help the U.K. citizen flee the charge, which brought a potential seven-year sentence. Anna had spoken of the real estate development she and her eye-candy husband, Kelvin Gorr, had made. Jonas had shown me her accounts—he didn't say what country they were in—with totals of $14 million. If Anna had some of that cash lying around the pig farm, it wouldn't be too bright to admit it. Judge Merchan, who already knew a lot more about the case than press and courtroom observers, sent her off to prison on Rikers Island.

On March 6, her co-counsel Peter Gleason tried to get her bail reduced. Anna had been brought from Rikers Island on the prison bus and into criminal court, wearing a zigzag-print wool jacket over black pants, accessorized with silver handcuffs. Maybe it was the reading glasses at the end of her nose, but I noticed for the first time how much Anna had aged since I first started working for her. The paranoia had taken its toll.

Gleason was a man of mystery. He had been a cop; he had been a fireman; he had run for City Council. But as a lawyer, he had never tried a felony case before. Not only that, but he offered up his TriBeCa loft as collateral for Anna's bail, even though he barely knew her. He even said Anna and her family could live in the $3 million spread, with a Japanese soaking tub in the guest bathroom, with him for the duration. When asked why, he explained that he and Anna "had a mutual friend."

In the courtroom sat famous private eye Vinnie Parco—the same Vinnie Parco whom Anna had called a "motherfucker" to me over the phone. Perhaps Parco worked for the "mutual friend"? Or maybe Anna thought Parco had done such a good job finding her that she wanted the best. Who knows. But after just fifteen minutes, Judge Merchan said he would have to study the idea of a defense attorney offering up his multimillion-dollar loft for a client and set a hearing on the matter. He ordered Anna back to Rikers.

nine lawyers, two hookers, and one beauty in cabo san lucas

Peter Gleason's offer of his loft for bail collateral was even more mysterious because Gleason wasn't even the chief lawyer on Anna's case. No, the court had appointed someone else to represent her after she said she was broke: respected defense attorney Richard Siracusa, who called Gleason "nothing but a hindrance."

At another hearing six days later, with Anna wearing the same zigzag jacket despite her extensive wardrobe, she made a legal maneuver that backfired with Judge Merchan. In a chaotic scene that the *New York Daily News* described as "bizarre," Gleason brought famous ponytailed civil-rights attorney and radio personality Ron Kuby before the bench to argue for Anna's right to jettison Siracusa and choose Gleason. Gleason stated, "It's going to take a very special lawyer to handle this matter."

Judge Merchan scolded, "Your client will not get preferential treatment here!" and ordered Anna back to Rikers.

Three days later, on March 15, it got even weirder when Anna replaced her two lawyers with two other lawyers. Not only did she get rid of Siracusa, she "fired" Gleason as well. Apparently money had been found to pay Gary Greenwald, a renowned "superlawyer" and the former mayor of Wurtsboro, New York, about half an hour away from Anna's farm in Monroe. His co-counsel was Elise L. Rucker, who is listed as having a house in Monroe.

Judge Merchan said that he and prosecutors had spent "hours" studying the legal and ethical issues raised by Peter Gleason offering his property as collateral while handling Anna's defense, but now that was all moot. When Greenwald tried to get Anna's bail reduced, Merchan refused, again pointing out that a woman with U.K. citizenship who had fled to a home she kept in Canada in 2008 was a flight risk. He set Anna's next trial date for three months hence on June 7.

Just two days earlier, Jaynie Mae Baker's perp walk had been a cakewalk. After the story broke in the *New York Post* of her February indictment, she flew from LA to Cabo San Lucas, the exclusive Mexican resort, with her sister Jessica. She claimed she hadn't known she was in trouble. But Jaynie Mae had one lawyer from the get-go, and he is among the crème de la crème of criminal defense attorneys: Robert Gottlieb, a former ADA under Morgenthau. Maybe Jaynie's rich boyfriend learned about him, I don't know; but his solid presence was in stark contrast to the courtroom circus Anna created by hiring a total of nine defense attorneys, which only seemed to annoy Judge Merchan.

Gottlieb told the judge that Jaynie Mae had no idea there was a warrant out for her arrest until she read it on Facebook in Cabo and friends told her that reporters were outside her apartment in Williamsburg, Brooklyn. Gottlieb made arrangements for her to turn herself in, and Jaynie Mae took her time thinking about it. She finally flew back on Saturday, March 10, to give herself up, but unfortunately, Customs didn't get the memo. Customs agents saw the warrant in her security file and detained her at Newark International Airport until Gottlieb had her sprung with a 10:30 p.m. cell phone call to Linehan.

The following Tuesday, paparazzi thronged Jaynie Mae as she was walked handcuffed into the New York State Supreme Court at 100 Centre Street, and her appearance caused one veteran cop to say, "She's the best-looking perp we've ever had in this court-house." At the arraignment, Charlie told Judge Merchan that he had had "numerous informants over the years who have discussed Ms. Baker's role in [Gristina's] operation." I was not one of them. I still believe the tailored and coiffed Jaynie Mae was only a participant in the aspirational part of Anna's business: linking wealthy men with young, beautiful women, but in a higher-class, legally loopholed way.

Despite Jaynie Mae's long stay in Mexico, Gottlieb got Judge Merchan to set her bail at $100,000, which was issued by famous New York bail bondsman Ira Judelson (who helped spring rapper Lil Wayne and International Monetary Fund chief Dominique Strauss-Kahn) after Jaynie Mae's boyfriend, Marcus Laun, put up his country house as collateral.

On March 16, investigators seized all the files of David

Jaroslawicz, who once sued quarterback Brett Favre and the New York Jets on behalf of massage therapist Christina Scavo for sexual harassment. He also sued the sultan of Brunei on behalf of former Miss U.S.A. Shannon Marketic, who claimed he'd held her against her will for thirty-two days and molested her in his 1,778-room palace. It was a story Anna had boasted to me on tape that she had given to "her friend at the *New York Post*."

Jaroslawicz was also Anna's next-door neighbor in Monroe, New York. His law office at 225 Broadway is listed in New York City Buildings Department records as the address for the LLC that owned Anna's brothel building. Jaroslawicz's office is also listed for the 881 Lakes Road LLC, which owns Anna Gristina's two-hundred-acre farm, located next to his.

"I think they're investigating whether there is some financial relationship," Jaroslawicz's lawyer Marc Agnifilo told Shayna Jacobs of DNAinfo.com, adding helpfully that the records documented Jaroslawicz's upstate real estate holdings. Since Anna and her husband, Kelvin, were also involved in real estate dealings, perhaps the records would show where Anna's money was figuratively "buried."

"I don't think at the end of the day that any of that's going to be criminal," Agnifilo told the website. Perhaps Jaroslawicz was just being neighborly. He was never charged.

Arrests had been made, potential evidence seized. Anna was locked up, and her trial wouldn't begin until October.

While at Rikers, Anna had an interesting inhouse neighbor: her former nemesis, Jason Itzler, the "King of All Pimps." Calling from a jailhouse pay phone with extra minutes he'd traded for cigarettes, the man who had once employed Ashley Dupré told Rocco Parascandola and Larry McShane of the *New York Daily News* that he believed Anna's law enforcement connections led to his arrest and to his escort service, New York Confidential, being shut down.

"When you control the hottest girls in the world, people kiss your ass," Itzler observed.

Itzler told the reporters that Anna was "dangerous, dangerous, dangerous . . . She sent three linebacker-sized guys to my office at New York Confidential. One had a gun. . . . This woman plays hardball. She's the most vindictive bitch ever in the escorting game."

Anna had told me in a call I recorded, "My guy sent two guys down to [Jason's] office to make it very clear to him." At every court appearance, Anna's husband, Kelvin Gorr, was bookended by two guys who looked like linebackers. They're the nattily dressed white men in the photos getting into an expensive SUV with him outside 100 Centre Street. You had to wonder if they were the ones who paid Jason the visit.

Anna could be sweet as Tupelo honey, but if you crossed her, she sounded like Scarface. This came out in a scoop by *New York Post* star reporters Laura Italiano and Jeane MacIntosh, who said that the DA's office had been investigating Anna ever since she had been arrested in 2004 for violent threats she made against one of the girls.

Anna had lost her temper with Jennifer Billo, a platinum-haired girl in her early twenties who was fighting with other girls over use of the East Seventy-Eighth Street place. Anna called her up and yelled, "I'm going down to the city, and I'm going to beat your head in with a baseball bat! I'm going to send someone right now! Right now, they are coming to your apartment! You'd better watch your back. You don't know who I know! I own New York!" Billo quickly reported Anna to police at the Upper East Side's Nineteenth Precinct. Anna then counter-reported Billo to cops for threatening to "put a bullet" in her head and those of her kids. Both ladies were arrested that summer, but then both dropped the charges. No matter: Anna had now put herself on the law enforcement radar. They soon found her connection to Jonas, and he was arrested in 2005 and released yet again.

Such stories during Anna's court case were rare. It seemed that most members of the New York media collectively seemed to feel that Anna's case was much ado about an activity that should be legalized anyway. As she languished in jail, emerging from time to time in court looking increasingly depressed, Anna became a media darling. Most of the newspapers, websites, and TV and radio news shows covering the case kept her in soft focus, talking about her four children, including a nine-year-old at home who was in the sole care of Anna's younger husband, Kelvin Gorr. Headlines went from calling Anna the "Millionaire Madam" to the "Soccer Mom Madam" and the "Hockey Mom Madam." Reporters and pundits talked about her being a mother of four and about her animal-rescue work on her farm. They lauded her loyalty for not naming her clients. They said DA Cyrus Vance and Judge Merchan should be ashamed for insisting upon and then setting such a high bail.

On April 27, soon after Anna had marked her two-month anniversary in jail, Kelvin and Anna's college-age daughters launched a website to try to raise her million-dollar bail: HelpAnna.org. Most of the press covered it sympathetically. "Perhaps it's time to rescue the rescuer," heralded the site. "Anna

Gristina-Gorr and her little son have dedicated their time to saving the lives of animals. . . . Anna provided a foster home for the Pig Placement Network. . . . The Pig Placement Network rescues pigs that are homeless or about to be slaughtered. Without the help of Anna, many animals would be left out in the cold.

"Our small family cannot afford the huge bail amount set for her—two million dollars! We are hoping that you will donate to help us pay for her bail, so she can live at home before the trial. We need our mom here.

"Anna Gristina-Gorr has not been convicted of anything. She awaits trial on Rikers Island, with an unjust bail, set higher than the charge against her warrants. The bail, set at a $2 million bond or $1 million in cash, is cruel and unusual. Real criminals, such as alleged rapists, murderers, and child molesters, have been required to pay less bail than she.

"Even more horrific are the conditions of the facility she is being held in. As if this wife and mother was a war-criminal, Anna is kept in solitary confinement, in a room where the temperatures exceed 100 degrees. Rats and roaches scurry all around her. The authorities humiliated her further by attempting to make her wear only a T-shirt and diaper. So much pain is being inflicted on a woman who has not been convicted, who according to America's own justice system deserves to be treated innocent unless proven guilty.

"Please help us fight this injustice; this insult to the American way of life. You can help by making a donation on this web site and by writing to your congress representative to protest. Any help is much appreciated!"

The "solitary confinement" cell that Anna was actually in was 180 feet long—bigger than most New York City apartments. A

Department of Corrections spokesman told radio reporter John Montone of 1010 WINS, "All of the allegations that are being made are untrue. This is not solitary confinement. It is not punishment. It is protective custody." The spokesman didn't say anything about the diaper.

Twelve days later, Anna was moving lawyers around like chess pieces yet again. On May 9 she fired "superlawyer" Gary Greenwald because he wanted her to take a plea deal. Some people speculated that she was afraid of getting deported back to Scotland. But Greenwald had also convinced the New York State Appellate Division to hear an appeal of Anna's bail on an expedited basis—a major legal victory. But Greenwald wouldn't be at the June 12 hearing to savor the fruits of his labor. Anna had replaced him with ponytailed civil rights and criminal defense lawyer Norman Pattis, who was perfectly respected—in Connecticut, where he was licensed to practice. Pattis was licensed to litigate in federal cases in New York, but not state cases. So Anna simply rehired Peter Gleason, who was licensed but had no felony litigation experience, and then she made the most bizarre personnel decision yet. She wanted Daniel Geller, son of the famous spoon-bending mentalist Uri Geller, on her legal team. Daniel was a lawyer, all right—in England. Perhaps she thought Daniel could bend the minds of the jurors.

Pattis represented her in front of the five Appellate Division judges, and their unanimous decision to slash Anna's $2 million bond to an eighth of that at $250,000 was his victory to relish. The panel gave Judge Merchan a little slap with a ruler, saying, "The amount of bail set by the trial court was unreasonable and an abuse of discretion." Their one caveat? Anna would have to wear an electronic ankle bracelet around the farm.

Pattis then scooted back downtown to the criminal court-house at 100 Centre Street to file a motion to get the whole case dismissed, claiming Charlie Linehan and the whole Manhattan District Attorney's Office was essentially trying to extort the big client names out of her.

On June 26, headhunter turned philanthropist Bonnie Lunt, who I'm pretty sure is friends with Anna's sister, Elizabeth, se-cured Anna's $250,000 bond. Ira Judelson didn't even need Peter Gleason's pad as collateral. Anna got out of jail on Rikers Island and went home to Monroe. She was free for now, albeit with an electronic bracelet on her ankle, and still facing a possible seven years in jail.

I wasn't proud of being part of where Anna was in her life right now. I also knew that each of us makes a choice, and she got herself where she was. I feel I was put in a position where I had to be a part of things that led to Anna's fall, but I was mad at her for the lies she told about her children. She went on national television and swore on her children's lives that she was innocent, and that was the one thing that I could not forgive her for. I knew the real Anna was in full play, and it was then that I stopped feel-ing sorry for her. She said on that first recording that if she was caught she would take responsibility, but it was all a lie.

It was all up to the Manhattan District Attorney's Office now. I thought my work was done and that I would get my life back. But then two things happened that shattered my sense of secu-rity. One, I started to receive strange phone calls from a man say-ing that Anna wanted to talk to me. I had pleaded with the DA's office on numerous occasions that I was worried they had put me in danger. A couple of times they acknowledged the level of dan-ger and went so far as to start the process of relocation, but then it would just stop all of a sudden. When I begged and pleaded, I would get an answer that "everything would be okay" or "just because she had been violent in the past didn't mean she would be in the future." They never helped me. Nothing had come out of it, but I felt like a sitting duck in hunting season.

And then, once I was sure that my time as an informant was over, the Manhattan District Attorney's Office wanted me to go undercover one more time.

one last job

Charlie Linehan called me and asked me to come down to Corruption headquarters. The Manhattan District Attorney's Office wanted to go after Anna Gristina's client, the global financier who had asked me to procure a young boy for him. Linehan wanted me to go undercover for him. Alone in my room, I sank to my knees, and wailed "No!"

The very idea of seeing him ever again revolted me. And I was scared. This guy had a lot to lose. He was high-profile on Wall Street, in Davos, on Paternoster Square. He had an image to protect in Manhattan and the Hamptons. He had a lot to lose.

But that day I had a visit with my beautiful, beautiful

daughter. I looked at her and thought, *What if somebody tried to molest her?* People who do that are the sickest people in the world. I wanted to help stop him.

Linehan wanted to bring this pervert down, and so did I. I called Charlie up.

"I'll do it," I said, and hung up.

Charlie had been better to me than his predecessors. But then something happened that changed my feelings about the entire Manhattan DA's Office for good.

I heard a commotion outside my apartment building one day and peeked out. There was a cavalcade of press: big TV cameras, the whole bit, jostling out there, including a crew from Geraldo Rivera's show. In March, it had come out that one of the girls had told investigators in 2007 that Anna had hooked her up with John Edwards. She told them that she and Edwards had had a paid sex romp when he was staying in New York at the Regency during a fund-raising tour for his presidential campaign. As was the usual modus operandi with politicians, one of Edwards's campaign aides knew Anna and hooked him up. The anonymous girl claimed Edwards had indeed been staying at the Regency in New York on the date she said she had sex with him there. He favored the Park Avenue hotel; interestingly, it was at the Regency in 2006 that he had met Rielle Hunter, the woman with whom he had an out-of-wedlock baby as his wife, Elizabeth, struggled with cancer. But his campaign spokeswoman denied the whole story.

It didn't help me one bit because no one knew who this girl was, and somebody falsely leaked to the press that I was the girl who had sex with John Edwards. I suspected it was Kristin Davis, the Manhattan Madam, my old boss. Kristin loved to go on *Geraldo* and had already done one guest appearance on Anna's case. I was furious that she would send press to my home, where my daughter would be visiting and where my neighbors would ask about the commotion.

And there was just one problem: although I have had my share of top politicians as clients, I did not have sex with John Edwards. As a fellow North Carolinian, I'm deeply ashamed of him. Of course, he didn't admit to fathering a baby while his wife struggled with cancer until 2010. But Anna simply didn't give me the job that day. She had fifty girls working for her. The *New York Times* reported that the DA's investigators had stopped using the girl as a confidential informant because she had developed drug problems. I don't do drugs and I never have.

But there was the fracas, at my front door. I frantically called Charlie.

"Charlie, you have to do something!" I cried.

"Rebecca, there is nothing I can do," he replied.

"Can't you send the cops to clear them out of here?" I wailed.

"Welcome to America, Rebecca. It's called freedom of the press," he said. I didn't like his sarcastic tone.

"Charlie, you have to get me out of here. I can't have Isabella see this. Don't you have an apartment somewhere that you've seized or something? If not, you're going to have to put me up in a hotel."

"Just sit tight, Rebecca. They'll go away."

I couldn't believe it. After all I'd risked for him, he was leaving me to twist in the wind. What if I needed major help later? The city and state don't have witness protection programs. At least the feds protect their confidential informants. But Charlie wasn't willing to go that extra mile. I felt betrayed. My trust was gone.

So now Charlie wanted something again. They wanted me to record the bad guy? Well, I was going to record Charlie too. I put a small tape recorder near the opening in the lining of my blazer, just as I had watched the techie do, when I went down to Corruption to talk about confronting Edward.

I went down to the SoHo office at the appointed time, and this conversation occurred:

DA Staffer No. 1: We'll need to put the device under your blazer. We need something other than what you're wearing; that won't work. Maybe something with a pocket. We'll open up a seam. Maybe bring us a jacket that's wool—not thin, with a lining. Come in tomorrow.

R: Tomorrow is Election Day. I can't do anything. I work the elections. I'm still a good citizen. You can't have this one. I don't want you to tear up this jacket.

DA Staffer No. 2: Maybe you can give us something that's not very luxurious.

R: That's the problem. All my clothes are expensive.

[Pause.]

DA Staffer No. 2: Well, that's the stuff that lasts, right? The good stuff.

R: Maybe I can go buy something inexpensive. You know, go into Bloomingdale's and—

DA Staffer No. 1: Bloomingdale's? Are you kidding me?

R: —or Ralph Lauren . . .

[Raucous laughter in the room.]

R: You're not going to ruin my Chanel . . .

[More laughter.]

Techie: I would also like to put a backup in your pocketbook.

R: We're not ripping up my pocketbooks again, are we?

Techie: We'll just add, like, a water bottle that will have a recorder in it.

Investigator: We have done surveillance on our target and we feel the best thing for you to do is approach him outside his office building as he exits. Security is very tight there. He won't want to make a scene in the lobby. It makes sense to approach him at his office because you could have Googled where he works, whereas if you show up at his house, it would be less plausible that you could have found that.

R: It's very stalkerish, I think.

DA Staffer No. 1: If you showed up at his house, he would be, like, "How did you find me here? You must be working with the DA."

So you approach him as he exits; you've been waiting for him, and we go from there. Hopefully he takes you into a coffee shop or bar or something to talk. We're thinking the best play is you tell him investigators have shown up at your door talking about this kid: "Look, I've been staying under the radar with this and so far nothing has happened. I know you're protected, you have a lawyer. But I don't know what I'm going to do here." And then kinda panic.

R: What if he goes past me and blows me off? What's the hook?

DA Staffer No. 2: I think the hook is "I've got the DA breathing down my neck about this case."

R: But why does he care?

DA Staffer No. 1: Because he was with the kid.

R: I need to say, "The DA is breathing down my neck about *you* and the kid."

DA Staffer No. 1: Say you have so far refused to talk to the DA about him, but now it's getting hot, and you need to strategize with him because you don't know what to do.

R: Should I say they pushed me and pushed me and pushed me and I need to make a choice: "Do I talk about you or should I not talk about you? So I need to talk to you about it."

DA Staffer No. 1 [role-playing]: "What am I supposed to do about this?"

R: "Do I talk about you or not?"

Female DA Staffer: You want a scenario where he thinks the ADA already knows all about him.

R [role-playing]: "You know Anna's trial is coming up and I don't know what's going to come out."

DA Staffer No. 1: You could even be more explicit and say: "They know about this incident with the kid. And I think I'm going to cop to it, because I'm not going to jail. And they're pushing me very hard for information on you. You don't know anything about me, but I have a lot to lose, and I imagine you do too."

DA Staffer No. 2: Start out weak and you could amp it up: "I'm not going to jail!"

R: And if he starts to walk away, I'll just say, "OK, I'm telling them everything tomorrow."

Linehan: It's unusual for us, because usually it's an undercover, but you, you know him better than anybody at this point. And you know how he's going to react. Grant it, it's a different setting, a different role.

Finally, I thought, *somebody is acknowledging what I had been doing for them.* I looked at Linehan and thought, *Maybe I can trust him.*

R: I'm going to tell him that I'm going to tell the whole world about him. What he wanted. What he had done. I'll tell him, "You will be so embarrassed in front of your family and friends. If I'm going down, you're going down."

Linehan: You have to talk about the kid. Be very specific.

DA Staffer No. 2: You have the main points about the kid. But if you start off easy, you go that way. If he resists—"I don't wanna talk to you"—then you go that way. "You know what, [Edward]?" You say his name. "This is what's going to happen. You're throwing me under the bus, I'm going to throw you under the bus. I could get arrested here." He has a lot to lose in terms of his status. There are people out there who are criminals who get arrested all the time. They live in that world. But people like [Edward], his world is really finance. He's got investors.

R [role-playing]: "Once [your clients] hear about your fetishes, and your interest in little boys, you're finished. They are not going to want you to touch their money. And people in jail do not like pedophiles. People are going to rape you in jail."

[Staffers freak out.]

DA Staffer No. 1: Whoa! I don't think you have to ratchet it up like that!

R: Our sessions were a million times worse than that. His sessions are . . . put it this way . . . for a week afterwards I
would be locked in my apartment, recovering. He is a very
sick man.

[Pause.]

Linehan: Why did you do it?

R: Money. Because he paid so well. Why do you think? He's got
a trust fund. Besides all the money he makes, he has family
money. I've got to go back to being that girl.

Linehan: If it gets to that point, go off on him, then. But that's your
fallback position. You're never going to have another chance
again.

DA Staffer No. 2: What happens if you meet him outside of work
and he wants to meet you another day?

R: He's not going to be seen with me in public.

DA Staffer No. 2: You have to say "I have to meet with you right now."

R [role-playing]: "We can go to your office."

Linehan: How far does the transmitter go?

Techie: We don't have the luxury of testing. I don't know how high
his office is. I'd like to put a recorder in also, just in case. If he
goes in a place where the walls are too thick.

It was becoming obvious that they all realized what I had
known about my involvement in any operation I had done for
them. They were worried they could not get to me or hear me
because the walls may be too thick for the transmitters to work
through. They were worried that they couldn't get to me quickly
enough. For the first time, they realized what kind of situation

they were putting me in *and* acknowledging it. I tried to convince myself it would be safe. I even tried to convince them.

R: He won't go into a bar. I'll be safe in his office.

Linehan: Will you be safe in his office? You're about to put him in a position where his whole world is in jeopardy. Have you known him to panic? In terms of being aggressive.

R: Never with me. I'm the one in control.

DA Staffer No. 2: That's a different scenario. Back into the office?

R: It's a location that's safe.

DA Staffer No. 1: What about his apartment?

Linehan: He's not gonna take her to his apartment.

Female ADA: What if you walked up to the park?

Linehan: That's not a bad idea.

DA Staffer No. 1: What about the Warwick?

DA Staffer No. 2: As soon as you text us the room number, we'll have an undercover out in the hallway.

DA Staffer No. 1: He's not going to want to have this conversation in a public place; he's not going into a bar; it's got to be in his office or at the Warwick.

DA Staffer No. 2: Say "They want to see me at the DA's office tomorrow."

R: Is it possible that Anna has reached out to [him], you know, that "if anybody tries to talk to you they could be an informant"?

Linehan: Yes, it's possible. But you have to let him know that the DA knows about the kid, like [role-playing]: "I don't know whether Anna told them, or whether they have the kid, or what."

R: I've gotta make it that he can't trust Anna. I have to convey that to him.

DA Staffer No. 1 [role-playing]: "Obviously, if you read the papers, you can see that Anna doesn't care. She's putting everything out in the media."

DA Staffer No. 2: You have to dirty her up. You have to point out that she's reveling in the media attention and that you and he aren't like that.

Female ADA: If he says, "Oh, they'll never find [the kid]," that's tacit acknowledgment.

DA Staffer No 2: We'll write out bullet points for you.

R: What if he has a meeting or something? Or a dinner?

Linehan: There is nothing so important that he'd have to go to that he wouldn't want to stop you from going to the media with the story that he got a blowjob from an eleven-year-old. I don't care if he's meeting with the mayor.

They wanted me to do it immediately. Edward traveled around the world a lot, and their surveillance showed that he had been working late nights at his office lately. They wanted me to do it within two days.

I was taken near his office in the surveillance van with several techies and detectives inside. They dropped me off about a block away, and I walked up to the dark glass skyscraper that was the headquarters for his company. I sat down on a bench in their public plaza and positioned myself to watch the banks of glass doors in the lobby. I waited there for hours. I was beginning to despair that he had flown off to some European capital. To make matters worse, it began to drizzle lightly. I stood under the cantilevered eaves of the building and called the lead detective; he said he didn't want me getting drenched. Just as he said to me, "OK, we'll pull the job for today,"

Edward appeared in the doorway with another man, exited, and turned right.

I walked at a quick pace to catch up to him, my heart racing.

R: [Edward], I have to talk to you!

Edward: I'm sorry, I don't believe I know you.

R: I apologize for interrupting you with your associate, but may I please have a private moment with you?

He looked frustrated and nervous, but his eyes gave it away. Without a doubt, he knew who I was. Although I was fully clothed and not in one of the many role-playing outfits he required in our past sessions, he couldn't miss me. He may have been in charge in his office, but he begged for me to be in charge of him outside of it. The real Rebecca is not that person. I am not a dominatrix. But I knew I would have to reclaim this role here and now to get him to listen to me.

Edward: How can I help you? I am sorry, but I honestly do not recognize you. [He was still trying to squirm away.]

R: You absolutely without a doubt know who I am. You don't fly me to Tokyo and spend tens of thousands of dollars on ridiculous sexual toys and beg for me to beat your p—

He stopped me. He reached for my arm as if to ask in a silent way for me to be quiet. He whipped his head around over to the man he had walked out of the building with to see if he had heard anything I had just said. He continued in a hushed voice.

Edward: What do you want? Money? Is that it? Are you here for money? You want me to write a check?

This man truly thought he could buy his way out of anything. He wasn't a regular client who asked for regular things. It was the main reason why he paid so much money for our time together.

R: NO! I don't want your money. Stop pretending you don't know me! Tell me you know who I am! Do not deny you don't know me as your domineering Ashley through Anna. Don't do that, or I will expose you to your work associates. I will tell the paper about you. I have people pressuring me because of you and us, and if you and I don't talk and help one another, I will save myself at your expense.

Edward: OK! I remember you. But what do you want? If you don't want money, why are you here?

He was defeated. He flashed me a look that I recognized from our sessions, the expression that told me, *You win and I am just a sad man who can't do anything. I am powerless.*
I was back in charge. And going in for what I came for.

R: Listen, you know very well why I'm here. The district attorney called me in, and they know about you and the boy. I didn't tell them anything or even affirm I knew what they were talking about. I merely sat there and listened and eventually asked if they were finished talking and asked if I was being charged with anything. They said they would be in touch very soon, and then they let me leave. So, here is what I am thinking. I am coming to you because there are only three people that know about this: me, you, and Anna. I know I didn't say anything about it to them, so it's either you or her that has screwed me over.

Edward: Hold on for a minute . . .

He walked over to his associate with the umbrella and said something to him, and then the man looked at me with a glare before he walked away. My target came back in a rush, looking a bit flustered this time, and stared at me dead in the eyes.

Edward: So, again, what is it that you want?

That is all he would keep asking for a while. I think he was in shock. Finally, he got smart. He looked me dead in the eyes.

Edward [looking me dead in the eyes]: Are you wired?

R: NO! And how do I know *you* aren't? Let's go somewhere so we can talk about this and figure out a plan of how to deal with the DA or lawyers or Anna. . . . I don't know and I will in good faith strip down and show you I am not wired!

It was my last move to show him that I was straight up on my own, and it worked. He calmed down instantly.

Edward: No, that's OK. No need for that. But look, the DA has not contacted me. I am not involved. So I think you should find yourself a good lawyer and deal with this.

R: Are you kidding me? They are coming for you! They knew everything, and they weren't getting it from me! All I can think of is Anna is sitting there in jail trying to make deals at our expense, and you and I are both going down. Look, you don't know this because I never told you, but I am a mom, and I am not going to jail and losing my child over something stupid you did. You and I need to work together on this. If we help each other out, we can make this go away. You have a lot of money. I don't. And NO, I do not want your money, but you can afford good attorneys. That is what you can help us both out with. An attorney can help figure out a way for you to deal with the DA when they come to you and charge you with some illegal sexual conduct with a kid.

Edward: Hey, look, they haven't come to me yet. Maybe they never will. I'll take my chances.

He started to walk away. I just looked at him and started shaking my head in disbelief. He looked back and said:

Edward: What? What's the problem?

R: Really? You are going to walk away from me? I come to you with crucial information that the freaking DA is coming for you and wants to take you down, and you say you are going to take your chances? Fine! I am not helping you! I am going to tell them everything, and you are going down. Go home. Kiss your family and tell them good-bye, because you don't have to worry about your chances. I can guarantee you that I will throw you under the bus to save myself. Whatever they want, I am going to give them! I don't care. I asked for your help, not money, and you treat me like trash. I am not the help. I asked to team up and keep one another out of trouble because you could not keep your hands off a child and who knows how many others. You make me sick. You make me want to throw up! I am going to do whatever it takes to keep predators like you off the street! I didn't do this job to make money so I could buy clothes and shoes and drugs. I needed it to save my family and put myself through school. I am not perfect, but I am not a monster like you! [He looked stunned.] So, run off to your meeting or dinner. Obviously making more money is more important than covering up your secret love for little boys giving you blowjobs!

Edward: Stop it! [He was breaking.]

R: No, *you* stop! The papers are going to love you, and, better yet, prison will *definitely* love you!

Edward rushed ahead towards a chauffered town car, face reddening and jaw tight. The driver jumped out and opened the door.

Edward shouted back at me, "I don't know what you're talking about. Have a good night."

He had obviously been expecting this ever since Anna's arrest. The conversation wasn't enough. I didn't pull the job off. We would have to get him some other way.

the madam goes free

Since Anna had gotten out of jail late on the night of June 26, she had been lying low on her spread, albeit while wearing a clunky electronic ankle monitor. Three days after Anna was sprung, Jaynie Mae made a solo appearance in court, where Judge Merchan told her that she and Anna would be tried together. Jaynie Mae's lawyer, Robert Gottlieb, didn't argue, saying he was fine with fighting the indictment in a team effort with Anna's lawyer, whoever that would be.

But then, on July 24, Anna got a clue that something was up with her co-defendant. Gottlieb filed a motion to get Jaynie Mae's case dismissed with the brilliant argument that, since the undercover officer just watched Maz Bottone and Catherine DeVries have sex, a crime didn't occur.

He told Judge Merchan that the secret video showed "the undercover officer meeting two other women at an apartment who eventually appear to engage in sexual contact with each other, but not with the undercover officer, which is confirmed by the video itself. The undercover officer apparently remains fully clothed, and merely observed the two women perform for him.

"If what occurred is considered prostitution, and what Ms. Baker allegedly 'promoted,' then every adult film director/producer and every owner of a strip club is guilty of promoting prostitution."

(Note to self: If you ever get busted, call Robert Gottlieb.)

On August 14, just two days before Jaynie Mae and Anna were to sit side by side at the defense table, Jaynie Mae blindsided her.

"Hooker Booker Strikes a Deal," trumpeted WPIX-TV.

"Jaynie Mae Baker has agreed to plead guilty to a violation," reported Janon Fisher and Corky Siemaszko in the *New York Daily News*, adding that "it won't leave a criminal record."

Gottlieb wouldn't tell reporters whether Jaynie Mae would take the stand to testify against Anna at trial in exchange for her get-out-of-jail-free card.

It was clear from comments made by Anna's lawyer Norman Pattis that Jaynie Mae hadn't even given Anna a heads-up call.

"I have every reason to believe we will be in court by ourselves on Thursday," said Pattis. "I am unaware of anything Jaynie Mae Baker can say that would hurt Anna Gristina. If she wants to say things to help herself, we understand. We regret she won't be sitting with us at the defense table."

Anna then made a statement that surprised me. "She's a good girl," she told the *New York Post*. "She doesn't deserve to be involved in this."

Here, even as Anna was maintaining that she was innocent, that she didn't run a prostitution ring, that her business was a matchmaking service, this statement seemed to be a tacit acknowledgment of her own guilt. In other words, Jaynie Mae was a "good girl"—but she was not.

Anna was the lone defendant in court August 16, but she wasn't alone. Anna thought it wise to have her young husband, Kelvin, bring her teenage son, Stefano, and nine-year-old son, Nick. No doubt she thought it made her look like the beleaguered mom. But at what cost to the boys as they heard the proceedings?

Her college-aged daughter, Suzie, also showed up, along with the private eye Vinnie Parco and the two hulky bodyguards whom Kelvin always kept around him. Was Kelvin afraid some of our tougher clients might show up to have a word with him? They didn't have to worry. Anna still wasn't talking.

"It ain't happening," her lawyer, Pattis, told reporters. "[Anna] is not cutting a deal. She is not cooperating. She is not interested in talking about the state's suspicions."

I had to wonder why Anna was being so stubborn. Did she fear more jail time? It was doubtful she would get the maximum seven years for a class-D felony, or even the four years that pimps sometimes got. Was she afraid of being deported back to Scotland? Or was she afraid of some of the clients?

But our clients had so much money, surely they could have rewarded her handsomely for her silence as they painlessly opened their wallets. If she went through the ordeal of a trial with her mouth shut, there were a lot of rich men out there who would be grateful. There was one in particular whom I truly felt she was counting on.

Kristin Davis didn't name names in court, either, but she pleaded guilty and had to hand over $2 million in profits after doing four months' time on Rikers. No, Kristin waited for the talk-show circuit to name names, including Eliot Spitzer and Dominique Strauss-Kahn. She admitted to "doing business" with ballplayer Alex Rodriguez.

Jaynie Mae and Jonas Gayer had flipped; so had Maz Bottone and Catherine DeVries. Not Anna. "We are going to trial," Pattis said at the hearing, and Judge Merchan set her trial date for October 15.

But then the judge said something unbelievable. Charlie stood up and told Judge Merchan that at the trial he might endeavor to introduce witness testimony and wiretap evidence "about other incidents not covered in the indictment."

Judge Merchan, perhaps annoyed at the prosecutors for their part in causing him to be reprimanded by the five-judge Appellate Division panel for setting Anna's bail too high, snapped at Charlie.

"This is a very narrow issue!" he warned. "This is going to be a very short case. I'm not going to allow this to get out of hand."

All the undercover work I had done and testified about in Judge Merchan's chambers; all the testimony of other girls and confidential witnesses who had not been arrested; all that Jonas Gayer, Anna's moneyman, had told the judge in his chambers— all of it was for *nothing*. All that was why Judge Merchan had set the bail so high—that, and because Anna was a flight risk. *None of that was going to come out, because there was only one charge on the indictment.* Why the hell did the prosecutors put me through so much if they weren't going to wait to build a stronger case before they indicted Anna? Why did they get Maz and Catherine to agree to take the stand and testify about all they knew about the business?

I was still stunned a month later when Anna went on the *Dr. Phil* show. Dr. Phil McGraw went up to Anna's farm and interviewed her at her round oak table, near a wood-burning stove and with views of the pastures through the glass doors. When he asked her if she was the madam of an escort service, Anna looked Dr. Phil in the eye and said with a straight face, "I have a matchmaking company I just started with a partner." When Dr. Phil asked Anna whether Maz Bottone and Catherine DeVries were call girls, Anna again looked Dr. Phil straight in the eye and said, "No."

I guess I wasn't a call girl working for Anna. I guess I was just working for a matchmaking company when I was having sex with rich men for money, of which Anna got a 40 percent cut.

Anna told Dr. Phil that the prosecutors wanted her to talk about two clients in particular, but she wouldn't. She also said that she had so little money "she could barely put food on the table." It's hard swallowing that when you're looking out the window at two hundred acres of meadow.

And while her attorney, Norman Pattis, who was sitting nearby and clashing with Dr. Phil, didn't allow her to answer questions about her case, Anna said she would take a lie-detector test and swear that she had never been a part of the business. Even though I had just heard her lie, that made me feel better.

Not two weeks later, on September 25, Anna was brought to the criminal courthouse in the prison bus from Rikers. She was in handcuffs, looking dowdy and defeated in a black sweater studded with silver. She was a far cry from the glamorous woman in furs with whom I'd once gone to Vegas with clients.

After four months on Rikers Island and three months lugging an ankle bracelet around the farm, she had had enough. Pattis had convinced her to "take the plea."

But Charlie Linehan also looked defeated. He rose and addressed the judge. "Over the years, the defendant made numerous claims that she had connections and influence in any number of city, state, and federal agencies, including the NYPD, the FBI, the DA's office, the governor's office, and Customs, among others," he said. "We have spent time investigating the defendant's claims, and we have not found evidence to support any of those claims.

"We are left with a straightforward promoting-prostitution case—a defendant who ran a brothel for many years who profited from the sex trade. That is all."

The ponytailed Pattis, who kept calling Charlie "my brother," said, "I don't expect anyone in this room to nominate Ms. Gristina for sainthood. But she has many good qualities, and among them is loyalty, despite the pressure that was brought to bear— not illegal pressure, but pressure nevertheless. We would recommend that if she were to enter a guilty plea that she be sentenced to time served. She is a first-time offender without a criminal record.

"I hope your honor will consider a plea of guilty to one simple count of promoting prostitution in July 2010."

Even the judge seemed in disbelief that it had come only to this. He seemed annoyed, and not just because Anna's husband, Kelvin, had brought their nine-year-old son into the courtroom to hear his mother called a trafficker in prostitution.

Judge Merchan scolded, "I have to say that I am certainly not pleased with some of Ms. Gristina's conduct during the proceedings. By way of illustration, I will say that I am not happy that Ms. Gristina's young child is in the courtroom."

Neither Anna nor Kelvin Gorr got the hint to have the boy brought outside, so Judge Merchan had to discuss the sex business in which Anna had engaged in front of him.

"Is it true, Ms. Gristina, that you arranged a sexual encounter with a man, then known to you as Anthony, between two prostitutes?"

"Yes," Anna answered meekly.

"If this had gone to trial," Judge Merchan continued, "you would face up to two and one-third to seven years incarceration, and I have promised you six months of a jail/probation split."

Anna would be on probation for five years.

"During probation, you must meet with a probation officer, have a job or go to school, not take illegal drugs, and submit to testing for illegal drugs. Do you agree?"

"Yes," she answered meekly again.

Judge Merchan then gave her a stern warning:

"Your guilty plea will subject you to deportation, and may interfere with any naturalization process. You may very well be deported as a result of this."

In quick succession in the next few weeks, Maz and Catherine, who had already flipped in May and were going to testify against Anna, were freed from having to go on the stand. They had a lot more to talk about than the one "girl-on-girl" incident. It turns out that, unbeknownst to each other, Anna had hooked them up separately with one of the wealthiest men in New York, a man who used his funds to influence elections. But for now, their testimony became moot. Maz left the courthouse with a jacket over her head, and Catherine's lawyer said she had been mortified by the experience, especially when her family found out how she had secretly been earning a living. She didn't throw a *schmatte* over her head, and so her face was all over the news. Catherine fled to California after pleading guilty to misdemeanor prostitution charges and getting off with no jail and no probation.

On November 20, two days before Thanksgiving, Anna was back in Judge Merchan's court for a perfunctory sentencing.

"Do you have anything to say, Ms. Gristina?" asked Judge Merchan.

"It's probably better that I don't, Your Honor," Anna replied. She would save that for *Dr. Phil.*

Anna was released, free to go, ankle monitor off, after being sentenced to the four months time served and five years probation.

That's it. That's all she wrote, as they say.

The DA claimed Anna had a lawyer friend who helped her invest and launder her money. "This is not that lawyer," said Jaroslawicz's attorney. Investigators seemed to find nothing in Jaroslawicz's papers and didn't bring charges against him. Jonas Gayer went scot-free, despite being taped by me with money launderers. They couldn't find Anna's money, though I had seen records of it on Jonas's computer. And despite Anna boasting on tape of her law enforcement connections, it came to naught. And somewhere out there, a very rich man is likely still pursuing his desires to have sex with a child.

naming names

Just before Christmas, Anna, who had said during the trial she'd rather "bite off her tongue" than name names, immediately told the press that she would start naming clients during a second appearance on *Dr. Phil*. The *New York Post*'s Page Six quoted Anna as saying, "There is going to be a giant name dropped—actually, a couple of them. Everyone's going to have to watch *Dr. Phil*. I will tell you that one of the names is high-level [NFL] management. Then there's an older [football] player who's still very well-known. Tune in to *Dr. Phil!*"

But all Anna's shilling for *Dr. Phil* had billionaires and other bigwigs who had been clients getting increasingly nervous, including one power player interviewed by top journalist Murray Weiss of DNAinfo.com. He admitted that Anna had hooked him up with a woman who worked as an interior decorator, as Maz did, after soliciting him via e-mail.

"I don't understand why [Anna] is sort of offering people up," the client told Weiss, who described him as a "50-something mogul."

"It has been an uncomfortable period for me, and I am sure for others, since all this began. But I can't figure out if she wants to sell books . . . or get on talk shows. . . . I think she feels she needs leverage, and it's a form of currency when you have something that is potentially sexy and salacious and worthy of a lot of curiosity. That may be the card she has to play.

"If it goes one way and she drops my name, there are relationships in my life that I will have to talk with. Not to be cliché, but I will not be open and trusting of someone who presents themselves one way and are not that way at all. It was bad judgment."

The power player said that he had had several "dates" with the pretty young decorator, yet he denied paying for sex. But in the very next breath he admitted that he had paid for her to fly home to see her family, and that he had helped pay her rent.

But as generically as Weiss had described the mystery man, New York cognoscenti soon figured out who the wealthy man with a well-known family was after a series of angry rants were posted by a commenter identified as "Anna Christina-Gorr." I clicked on the posts, and they linked back to Anna's usual Facebook page. In her rants she said the client's attorney was megalawyer Ben Brafman, and she knew that Weiss knew Brafman. She knew the client had made political donations, and why he made them.

One post read like a populist rallying cry: "And suddenly the Scared Mogul with all his Billions . . . now he is taking the 'I-knew-nothing' road. 'I'm a victim.' REALLY N.Y. do you believe that? People of N.Y., ask why he never came forward . . . to tell his story of events and how innocent everything was. I'd have had all charges dropped if he did come forward . . . and do the proper legal thing to clear my name since it was all SO INNOCENT on his part. But instead [I] sat for 4.5 months in Rikers."

An hour later, "Anna Christina-Gorr" posted this: "Really, it looks a lot like he is trying to worm out of any legal and moral responsibility due to his Billionaire lifestyle. . . . This is damage control in case I do a book with names. Well, let's look at his history in both coasts with paper trails, texts, phone records, voice messages and emails, and let him be the first to stand and be tried as a man involved in this, and I will be happy to bring forth women who may have a very different story than his 'poor-me' version. MONEY WON'T BUY YOU OUT OF THIS ONE, as I plan on sitting in the Bonnie Island of Scotland where I will have total freedom with solid verifiable facts to write all I have uncovered."

The comments were taken down by DNAinfo.com almost immediately.

Judge Merchan gave Anna permission to fly out to LA to tape her second appearance on the *Dr. Phil* show, which aired in February 2013. Dr. Phil McGraw was not happy that she had denied during her first appearance in September that she'd ever promoted prostitution, only to plead guilty to doing so not two weeks later.

"You were either lying then, or you're lying now," Dr. Phil

said. "You can't say 'yes' then and 'no' now. There are not versions of the truth. You're insulting my intelligence."

Anna then had the nerve to say, "I've never owned an 'escort service.' That's below the level of what I was comfortable doing. . . . But, yes, older men met with younger, beautiful women with the expectation of having sex. . . . I knew it was going on, but it was not something anyone ever talked about."

Dr. Phil: "What's the most money you ever made in a month off of this?"

Anna: "I think a bumper of a month was like Super Bowl weekend. It was amazing. I made a lot of money."

Dr. Phil: "So for weekends, this doesn't sound like people test-driving girls for a long- term relationship, it sounds to me like they come in for a weekend and you hook them up with a hooker."

Anna: "Yeah."

Dr. Phil: "So you were a pimp?"

Anna: "If that's the way you want to call it, yeah."

Anna admitted to having a "global roster of fifty to one hundred girls," but said she had an "active database" of ten to fifteen girls at any one time.

Dr. Phil brought up her claim that she was going to name some of her clients on his show. He said he wasn't interested in divulging any names, since "I don't think you have credible information."

Anna claimed she took the plea deal to protect people who had enemies in the Manhattan District Attorney's Office.

She said there was a man who "was like a father to me." She said that, even though she had pleaded guilty to protect him, he wouldn't talk to her now. She started to cry. Dr. Phil wasn't having any of it. He said, "You're trying to make yourself out to be a *victim*?"

I have my suspicions as to who that is, and I will say that, yes, if it is that person and he did leave her stranded, I do feel badly for her. I knew him, and I know how very close they were. I would be equally hurt.

a whole new life

As for me, I continue to fight for my daughter, though it's really just down to legal technicalities now. She is with me a lot of the time, and her father and I have begun talking again, for her sake.

I left the escort business for good a long time ago. I went back to school to become a forensic psychologist. I became a student at the John Jay College of Criminal Justice. I decided to work on the right side of the law instead of the wrong side. I want my daughter to be proud of me.

I've been in compromising situations. I understand the

low end and the high end of the business. I understand the madams—and the clients. I understand the young women who turn to prostitution for whatever reasons they have, and then want to get out.

Forensic psychologists are often called in to decide whether defendants are of sound mind, and whether they're telling the truth. I found that a lot of girls in this business lie so much. I guess that's how they cope. And sometimes you have to lie in order to keep that part of your life a secret. Regardless of the reason, it is very stressful.

I have gotten very involved with my community and was even elected to the Community Education Council, and then the council elected me first vice president. I have lobbied in Albany against budget cuts for public education in New York City. I have stood in front of numerous groups, whether at a press conference at the courthouse or meetings within the community discussing land use, new schools, budget allocation, or school rezoning. I took chances that I would be recognized and somebody would say, "You are that girl who is a prostitute!"

I took that chance because I am not that girl for life. It was a short period of time in my life that certainly changed it forever. Some people will never be able to handle my truth. It doesn't matter how good a person you are—there will always be someone who judges you, and it is that person for whom I feel sorry. I learned along the way that those who judge are the ones with the biggest secrets and the most fearful that they will come out.

I am often asked by those who don't know me very well why I chose to tell my story. The question always brings to mind a simple line from the movie *Cloud Atlas*. When asked why she embarked on her chosen path, the main character, Sonmi-451 states, "If I had remained invisible, the truth would have stayed hidden. I couldn't allow that to happen."

There are so many truths that had to be told, yet one thing inspired them all: my beautiful Isabella.

acknowledgments

It would be impossible to thank and express appreciation to each person who has influenced my journey and reminded me to "keep my chin up," as my Pop would say, during the difficult times and celebrate life's incredible moments.

My deepest gratitude to my incredible literary agent, Frank Weimann, who sat down at a table with me one day and listened to my story, and from that moment on had faith in me and in this project. Thank you for getting me through this!

My sincerest thanks to my editor, Emilia Pisani of Gallery Books, who has patiently dealt with me during every stage of this project and, more importantly, worked closely with me on writing subject matter that was difficult on many levels. Also, to my publicist, Stephanie DeLuca of Gallery Books, for making sure *Call Girl Confidential* has a future once released. And to Simon & Schuster for working with me for these many long months.

To my family, thank you for your support and love and understanding. I have never been the easiest one to decipher, but I have always had my reasons for what I do. Mom, you are an amazing grandmother, and it has been wonderful to watch my daughter grow up so happy visiting with you. Thank you for creating those memorable moments. Aunt ML, our special bond is something I value deeply and never take for granted. To Saint Bridget, who loves gentle round barrel-makers, the thought of writing anything to thank you makes me cry. You are my everything: my parent, my sister, my best friend, and the most incredible person. Your brilliance is not lost on me, and I am glad the rest of the world has caught up and sees it too. To say thank you would be but a drop in the bucket of what I owe you. My heart will always be so full of love and gratitude.

Thank you, Timmy, for being the brother I never had. We have always been able to count on you for anything and everything, but most of all for your unconditional love. You inspire, you love, you give, you teach, yet you ask for nothing in return.

Oh, Shahana. I don't think there will ever be enough room to thank you for all you are and have done for me and my daughter. Our souls were connected long before we met, and the place you hold in my heart is so deep and powerful that nothing I can say here will be good enough to honor and justify the friendship we have. So, simply put: thank you for your constant love and support. I am . . . because of you.

Steve Caton, long before the days chat rooms ever existed, you were one of my dearest friends in college and the person I knew I could confide in without any judgment. This still holds true today. My life could be a complete disaster if you were not a constant support. I may never be able to cheer for your college team, but I will love you forever!

A fun night would never be complete without my daughter, Twizzlers, a good movie, and you, Jason Baron. Jason, I will forever be grateful that I met you at your own birthday party all those many years ago. You redefine friendship. You continue to surprise me with your fierce loyalty and love, and it continues to grow with us. Whenever we're at a party and there's a piano bench, you can be sure I'll be saving that spot next to me only for you! I truly love you, and your support while writing this book has been absolutely essential to its completion. Thank you for being family.

Living in solitude all those years to keep my secret safe meant being alone on holidays when I didn't have my daughter. But, Virgina Reiff, letting me spend Thanksgiving with you and your family was the most impressive gesture a friend has ever made. Who knew you would end up reading draft after draft of this manuscript, helping me and giving me advice on how to make it better? You are an amazing writer, a fantastic friend, an incredible party host, and the best doggy mom ever!

Andrew Arora, you always tell it like it is, and you always let me cry on your shoulder when my heart has been broken. Our conversations are priceless, and I have never been more grateful for ex's and roommates than I am now. And whenever you are ready for season two of *Hannibal,* wait for me! (Wait, *is* there a season two?)

To Bruce and Victor, having you in my life taking care of me during the most physically challenging times ever, I could never thank you enough. I started out as just another client you represented. Now you are both my family, and I love you dearly. I just want to know, though . . . when ARE we going to the Bahamas?

Friends show up when we least expect it, and Lauren Testa, it doesn't matter if I need to talk about relationships, I need a last-minute tan, I want to just text, or whatever, you never ever let me down. How you can always be there for everyone else is inspiring. And thank you for sitting in that hospital room for hours on end. Thank you for showing up for everything. You are the friend everyone can depend on for a favor, yet probably rarely has the favor returned, and I have never heard you complain. You simply ask, "What else can I do? Is there anything you need?" Happiness is possible because of you.

During the most horrible period of our lives, from the bottom of my soul and heart I love you, Laura and Randy, for taking care of my daughter. To trust someone with my child is the most difficult thing someone could ask of me, but you became family. I'm grateful you didn't look at her as a job, and I am forever in debt to you for that.

To Jason Y, a thank-you that you are not expecting, since we no longer speak to each other, but one you deserve. I won't say that either of us was great relationship material for the other. However, your companionship during the most tumultuous period of my life gave me a source of stability each day, and I looked forward to cooking dinner, watching our favorite TV shows, and of course, going on fantastic vacations. Hopefully this book will provide some answers to a lot of questions you probably had back then. Thank you.

To my personal team, Joseph Ungoco, Stephen Ciuccoli, William Miranda, and Yuki Yamazaki: thank you for "fixing me up" and pulling off miracles in Connecticut. Stephen, your work is outrageously amazing. Joseph, who knew that teaching a few people about poll sites would lead us here? To be able to trust is nearly impossible for me; however, you are the most fun, laid-back, stylish, and incredibly smart friend that I am so lucky to spend so much of my time with now. Having you by my side makes it all seem so easy. Thank you for taking away the stress from the entire project.

And to those precious souls who have passed on . . .

I praise God for the friendship I had with Nancy Ann. Nancy, you were one of the most loyal friends I have ever had, and it is because of you I was blessed with the most important relationship in life, my daughter. You always believed in me, even when I didn't. And to Christian Myler, an elite Special Operations Marine who proudly served this country in Iraq during combat and tragically passed away just sixteen days before Nancy. You were and always will be the true love of my life. I have felt your disappointment in my actions and also your praise for finally doing the right thing. You are a constant guide in my heart. More recently, I miss my amazing grandfather. I am grateful for all the love and support you gave my daughter, her father, and me. Everyone would have the most incredible life if they had a grandfather like you. Again, unconditional love and no judgment for a young, scared, unwed pregnant girl is like winning the lottery, and I kept winning with you every single day. Your support helped raise her to become the most beautiful, talented, smart, and caring person I know. And lastly, to my father: although childhood may have been very strict, spending the last couple of weeks of your life with you are moments I would not trade for anything. Talking about the past, even though I don't think you heard me, somehow seemed to set everything straight and make everything better. Thank you for those last moments, and thank you for letting me hold your hand while you left this life and went to the next. I love you, Daddy.

And to my daughter: your birth changed everything in life for the better. You have parents that love you tremendously and believe in your amazing gifts and want nothing but love and happiness for you. You are the most beautiful, intelligent, talented, and loving human in this universe. I am so proud of everything you are and will become. Thank you for never complaining, for never giving us a hard time, and for innately treating people with respect. Even during challenging times, you always prevail because you never give up. You know how much I love you, and it is the biggest love my soul has ever felt. You make me want to work harder at becoming a better person and a better mother each day.